The New Road

For a Naive Scientist and Everybody Else

Are You Ready for the New Road? ... since you are on it anyway.

and the Paradigm

Peter Dodd Cooper, DSc, PhD

'There's a battle outside and it's ragin' ...
Please get out of the New (Road) if you can't lend your hand,
for the Paradigms they are a'changin' ...'
With apologies to Bob Dylan, 1963.

Foreword by Marjorie Hines Woollacott

Copyright © 2022 (Peter Dodd Cooper)
All rights reserved worldwide.

No part of the book may be copied or changed in any format, sold, or used in a way other than what is outlined in this book, under any circumstances, without the prior written permission of the publisher.

Publisher: Inspiring Publishers,
P.O. Box 159, Calwell, ACT Australia 2905
Email: publishaspg@gmail.com
http://www.inspiringpublishers.com

 A catalogue record for this book is available from the National Library of Australia

National Library of Australia The Prepublication Data Service

Author: Peter Dodd Cooper
Title: The New Road and the Paradigm
Genre: Non-fiction
ISBN: 978-1-922792-12-9

FOREWORD

Peter Dodd Cooper's book, *The New Road and the Paradigm,* is both a spiritual memoir and a series of scientific articles on his own exploration of the nature of consciousness and of reality itself. As a scientist, he brings credibility to this book with his credentials from a long and productive scientific career. From this vantage point, he then explores topics that don't fit into our current materialist paradigm, looking deeper to see if he can find more satisfying answers. After exploring the mysteries of quantum physics, the nature of the mind, and psychic phenomena, he concludes his exploration by saying, "Experiencers tell us that reality is that realm outside Plato's cave, where colours are brighter and Oneness with everything is self-evident." As a fellow scientist who has also explored through meditation and inquiry the nature of reality beyond the Plato's cave of materialism and has discovered a Oneness within all beings, I heartily agree.

~ Marjorie Woollacott, Professor Emeritus, Institute of Neuroscience, University of Oregon, and author of *Infinite Awareness: The Awakening of a Scientific Mind*

DEDICATIONS

To Barbara, David and their loving and loved Soul Group,
to traditional societies who have much to teach
those who care to listen
and to all others who sincerely wonder
what on earth they are doing here
and if it matters anyway.

CONTENTS

Copyright ii
Foreword iii
Dedications v

Prologue – The 'How' of this Book xiii
   Why the Author and This Book Are (Firmly)
   Post-Materialist xiv
   Epiphany xvii
   Subsequent Years xxvi
   Concluding Thoughts xxvi
   References xxvii

Chapter 1. Universe of Maya – A Material Universe with Cryptic Meaning 2
   Energy is a Basic Fact of Nature 3
   Consciousness is a Basic Fact of Nature 4
   Time is a Basic Fact of Nature 5
      Illusions of the First Kind –
      The Five Senses Determinant 7
      Illusions of the Second Kind –
      The Quantum Determinant 9
      Illusions of the Third Kind –
      The Curriculum Determinant 11
      The Party Line from Science on the Origin
      of the Universe – Another Illusion? 12
   Discussion 13
   Conclusions 15
   References 16

Chapter 2. A Reverse-Paradigm Creed for the Twenty-First Century: Why Many Scientists Still Have the Cart Before the Horse 20
   Is There a Relevant, Simple Message from Science? 21

    The Finely Tuned Universe..22
    Paranormal (Psychic) Phenomena 22
  Is There a Relevant, Simple Message from Religion?.......25
    Atheism...26
    Christianity...27
    Islam..28
    Hinduism...28
    Buddhism 29
    Newer Aspects 31
  Is There a Relevant, Simple Message from Philosophy?...31
    Conclusions from Science...34
    Conclusions from Religion 35
    Conclusions from Philosophy 36
  Synthesis 36
  References...37

Chapter 3. A Real Fifth Dimension? 40
  The Design Question – The Material Universe 41
  The Design Question – The Machinery of Life 42
  The Hoyle–Wickramasinghe Version of Cosmic
  Cometary Biology..46
  Quantum Entanglement 50
  Quantum Tunnelling 50
  Non-Local Consciousness – The Quantum Observer
  Effect on Wave–Particle Duality......................................51
  Psychic Phenomena (PSI)..52
  Discussion 55
  Conclusions...58
  References...59

Chapter 4. Purpose: A Slow Dawning for Us All?.............64
  1. Debunkers Debunked...66
  2. The Turin Shroud 70
  3. Reincarnation 74
  The 'Why' Question...77
  Conclusions...78
  References...80

Chapter 5. Our Great Leap Forward and Us – Right Now 84
    The William James Legacy 88
    First Nations Australians' record keeping 91
    Ko-Ko's dilemma 93
    References 96

Chapter 6. Quo Vadis, Human Intuitive Mind? 100
    The Left Brain – Right Brain Conundrum 101
    The Big Five Personality Test and
    McGilchrist's Designations 102
    The Myers-Briggs Personality Test and
    McGilchrist's Designations 104
    Where Else Does Intuition Serve? 106
    Discussion 108
    Conclusions 110
    References 111

Chapter 7. The Importance of Sharing for Humanity and its Planet 114
    Is There Something Within Worth Sharing? 115
    Sharing among the Madding Crowd 115
    Sharing in the Tribe 116
    Is The Cosmos Trying To Share Something With Us? 119
        Are UFOs Real or Are They Just Science Fiction? 121
    Conclusions 125
    References 126

Is There a Meaning to Life for Humans? 129

Epilogue – The 'Why' of this Book 130

Acknowledgements 131

About the Author 132

LIST OF FIGURES

Figure 1. Bloodstains on Peter's underpants from
23 May 1981..xxv
Figure 2. Diagram of a feasible self-sustaining material
universe. This model requires three testable
postulates, as explained in the text quoted. 12

LIST OF TABLES

Table 1. Radiocarbon dating of the Turin Shroud. 71
Table 2. Summary of McGilchrist's designations
 and the OCEAN Personality Test. 102
Table 3. The sixteen Myers-Briggs types rearranged to
 reflect brain orientation..105

> Intuitive Mind is a sacred gift,
> Rational Mind its faithful servant.
>
> We now often worship the servant and deride the divine.
>
> Bob Samples, 1976, interpreting the views of Albert Einstein

This is not a tract to tell you how to live your life.
That is your business.
Planet Earth is approaching a tipping point.
That is everybody's business.

We are being nudged to wake up to our inheritance.
This book interprets the massive database of scientific literature that tells us what makes up the universe we live in.

It reveals a paradigm that is not the old materialist one.
The universe is made of Mind-stuff, and its essence is loving consciousness.
Realising that tells you how to live your life.

It was not meant to be easy, just non-negotiable.

Prologue – The 'How' of this Book

This is the true story of a life sciences researcher who, soon after his first half-century on Earth, was dramatically shown that he had got the structure of the universe all wrong. It was a spiritual revelation, and it *mattered*. Now, over four decades later, he realises that this has been quite clear from the scientific record all along. This book attempts to show why and why it matters.

Where we can observe the details, the material universe is so cleverly dovetailed together that this book assumes that all its aspects must 'make sense' in an overall plan. As written here, it appears to do just that.

Dear reader, if you have an alternative view, please be sure that all its aspects 'make sense' too.

Most of his colleagues have still got it all wrong; that is their business, of course. However, it matters to other people because people generally assume that scientists know what they are talking about, especially eminent ones. Scientists have a leadership responsibility of which they are often unaware. Leadership is still lacking because most scientists are still stuck in materialist mode [1].

True, there can be acute discomfort in using a dissecting microscope on spiritual matters, which are sacred matters, Heart-stuff. But, as in any life decision, Heart-stuff must be reconciled with Mind-stuff: the two must align, or one or the other must be in error. This is how science works, intuition and rational mind together. We have been given both and should use both. Humanity is at a critical level of spiritual development where it badly needs both.

The substance of the following reflective essays was published separately and seriatim in the journal *EXPLORE:*

The Journal of Science & Healing between 2015 and 2019. It was unexpected that each was acceptable for publication, helped by peer review and editorial correction. The real surprise was their logical sequence of sorts, as there was no prior intention of a planned series. They seemed to have followed serendipitous reading and then an urge to write (his trade as a science researcher) on a subject he was passionate about but had no apparent qualification for (sometimes, this is an advantage). Indeed, they were more like mediumistic channelling, guidance from spirit, shaped by the transcriber's interpretation of the science involved.

It turned out that the New Road is none other than the Old Road in the shape of Huxley's *The Perennial Philosophy*, Schucman's *A Course in Miracles* or Walsch's *What God Said: The Core Thousand Words* but directly derived from a science that is prepared to examine all the data, which it must. These data are now firm enough to qualify fully as hard science. Of course, the theoretical background is still lacking – for example, we do not know how psi works – but progress is being made, with a little help from a surprising source of friends.

WHY THE AUTHOR AND THIS BOOK ARE (FIRMLY) POST-MATERIALIST

A Slice of an Autobiography

(Some names have been initialised to protect privacy)

To cut to the point, I believe that I am a reincarnation of my maternal grandfather George McDouall.

I resemble my Grandpa McDouall in general build, face shape and posture (in some photos). There's no surprise there; the genetics are quite close, and our hair parting is very similar. But in the comparison below of George and me, the resemblance in body stance is almost uncanny.

Prologue – The 'How' of this Book

George (1900).   Peter (1949).

The surprise is that I have two inguinal hernias. The left is the usual one in males (a protrusion of abdominal adiposities into the inguinal canal), but the right one is unusual. It coincides with the typical location of a McBurney incision used in appendectomy operations, practised in the United Kingdom since the 1890s. The incidence of such a hernia in those who have had an appendectomy is less than 1%; it must be vanishingly small in those like me without that operation. During my recent (2015) operation for bowel cancer, the surgeon was quite interested in this anomaly (using the words 'McBurney point') and attempted to draw the muscles together but told me the stitches 'just tore out of the muscle tissue'. I infer that they were congenitally weak or absent.

Since my Grandpa died because of appendicitis, and since there is evidence from the work of Ian Stevenson MD [2] that the new body can carry evidence of the mode of traumatic death of the previous personality in cases of apparently confirmed reincarnation, I am persuaded that my higher self is likely that of my Grandpa (a compliment for me). Death from a ruptured appendix comes ultimately from septic shock – the sudden release of many live and putrefying bacteria carrying endotoxin, a powerful poison. It would certainly explain my eight-year-old's insistence on science, my early enthusiasm for bacteriology and antibiotics (especially penicillin) and my gratuitously easy, parachuted entry into international science, with an honours degree in science, a PhD, a paper in the top journal *Nature* and an effectively permanent academic post, all before my 23rd birthday.

At age 21 (1947), a job was past timely. After applying to four chemical firms, I was offered only one, and I started at Distillers Co. Research Labs in Epsom Downs in September to improve their penicillin and streptomycin isolation. (Anyone can distil gin; it is the brewing that takes know-how.) Penicillin chemistry again was exactly right for my next task.

After nine months at Distillers Co. Research Labs and feeling a need to publish my efforts, I happened on an ad in *Nature* for a research assistant to Sir Alexander Fleming (the inventor of penicillin) at the Wright-Fleming Institute, St Mary's Hospital. I expressed confidence in doing the work and added 'to our mutual advantage'. The obvious impertinence of this felt right. My supervisor, Derrick Rowley, said years later that this was noted as the sort of cheek he might use himself; it soon came true for us both.

Starting June 1948, I was given a complicated way to measure bacterial uptake of radioactive penicillin to see how the drug worked. Derrick then took off for six weeks' honeymoon leaving me to it. I found a better, much simpler assay method but had to risk it all by purifying half of our precious but half decayed drug stock, which I was quite skilled at from the Distillers Co. Research Labs job. All penicillin-sensitive bacteria then took up the tracer by a set amount, while resistant ones did not. When Derrick returned, he was astounded to find the problem solved; my predecessor had spent an entire year trying to solve this problem but had got nowhere. This became the first paper (published in 1949 in *Nature*) in a series that showed that penicillin bound covalently to a component of the delicate waterproofing lipid layer that synthesised the tough contiguous cell wall located just outside. One can count the unusual synchronicities involved in this sequence of events; it was all suggestive of guidance.

I took to research naturally, with a 'nose' for stories like a journalist and needing little supervision so Derrick could finish his medical degree part time.

Thursday's Child. The synchronicities did not stop there. Because of World War I, my parents could not marry until 1919. My brother Tony was born in 1922 but only lived two days after a difficult birth. My mother, a trained gymnast, was told that her muscles were too tight, and she would never bear children. After that blow, one can imagine their feelings when, three years later, they found that medical science could now provide safe Caesarean deliveries. The surgeon's name was Mr Dodd (later FRS). Since my mother's much-loved only sister, Ethel Mary, was nicknamed Dodd, this synchronicity would be meaningful to both my parents; Aunty Dodd had died in the flu epidemic of 1918. Hence my middle name. I was delivered by appointment in Bolingbroke Hospital, Wandsworth, at 11 am on Thursday, 22 July 1926. Why this eminent surgeon did not use one of the great London teaching hospitals is a puzzle. Just 21 years earlier, my grandfather George McDouall died in that same small, suburban hospital.

But first, I was compelled to educate myself spiritually.

EPIPHANY

It all began in Scotland in October 1978, when I was 52. At least, that was when it all began to make sense. My wife at the time, Mary, son David (aged 11) and I had just completed a round trip, self-drive tour of Northern Italy, from Genoa through Pisa, Siena, Assisi, Milan and other places crammed with history. We mostly stayed in pensiones, and in one, owned and run by two ageing sisters, one asked about my job. She was most interested in my standard reply of 'medical research', but the virology details disappointed her (in hindsight, they were rubbish at that time). She replied, 'Ah, signor, what about the can-sair!' What about the cancer, indeed? This was clearly the terror for her age group.

A small digression. By accident, really, I had a year or two before become chairman (a voluntary position) of the Australian Capital Territory Cancer Society, now ACT Cancer Council. It turned out very necessary for the Cancer Society, but that is another story. Another story is the history behind this article, which I should explain in part. My day job was as a fairly conventional medical researcher, which, until I fully retired in 2014, I was careful to protect by not appearing scandalously New Age. Such is academia. I have published some 160 papers in peer-reviewed journals (mostly with few collaborators), trained a number of PhD students and occupied a tenured academic position. Of these papers, the most recent five [6,7,8,9,10] were published in the journal *EXPLORE: The Journal of Science & Healing*. These I developed into this book. I always treasured academic freedom, declining senior management and head of department positions.

My conventional contributions were often ahead of their time; I sometimes became the world expert for a season, but then melded into the rich compost of scientific endeavour as is natural. My fields of study were: (1) the site of action of radio-penicillin, (2) the genetic structure of the poliovirus including the classification of animal viruses, (3) the design of vaccine adjuvants as the basis of anticancer treatments and (4) the structure of the universe. My aim was always focused on people. My name is on four granted vaccine adjuvant patents, all expired except the last one, which is still in play against SARS-CoV-2 but I have no pecuniary interest in it.

Returning to the main story. Mary and David had returned to Canberra. This study leave, as an invited Visiting Professor to the Virology Institute of the University of Glasgow, was to be my last foray into viruses and the beginning of a difficult, painful and confusing five years for many of us. My job in Glasgow was to give seminars and lectures to researchers, staff and students, talk personally to them, help them to make me understand their projects and find problems and suggestions. On weekends, I was free to explore the nearby Highlands by car. I had ancient family links to this beautiful but economically difficult region. Meanwhile, I was in a form of mental freewheeling about research directions and indeed what Life was all about.

By chance, Anne, a Scottish country dance friend from Canberra (who had the same name as my youngest daughter) had just returned to Scotland, her home in Allowa, the birthplace of Robert Burns. She was also a family friend, a senior primary-school teacher and a committed Christian. She invited me to a Scottish country dance social in Stirling, close to Glasgow, and I took her on a drive to the Highlands. Walking there, I explained I was a wistful agnostic and could not just 'believe'; I questioned what faith was and why. I realised the 'why', the antithesis of faith, was crucial. The reply was disconcertingly simple. 'Talk to God,' she said. 'If you genuinely want to know, He will answer you.' (Later I did, and I really meant it.) Anne also mentioned that there would be a commemorative service at the mainly thirteenth century Dunblane Cathedral the following Saturday, and why don't I stop by. I said I certainly would.

At the turnoff to Dunblane, a bit late and thinking, 'Nah, they will have started and it's only a church service,' a voice thundered in my head 'O YE OF LITTLE FAITH!' Stunned and somewhat shamefaced, I said aloud 'OK then,' and duly turned off. This was an example of clairaudience, fairly common apparently, and which I interpret as my guardian angel at work[1].

The Dunblane Cathedral, no longer a bishop's seat, was the size of a largish English parish church – very beautiful mid-gothic with a long narrow nave. The crowded service had indeed started and, as my rear was just hitting a seat at the back, I was called loudly from the pulpit: 'PETER!' Boy, did I listen! This is an example of a true synchronicity, a really meaningful coincidence. Of course, he was just announcing the day's lesson using an amplified speaker, a familiar piece from the first book of Peter. After the very pleasant service, I travelled to Oban to visit the MacDougal family seat of Dunolly, then to Mull and Iona.

On the way, I was hailed by a jolly, rather hippy (beads, etc.) girl in her thirties. I took her to Oban; she lived on the Isle of Mull and was returning from a little place called Findhorn on the Moray Firth. (There, in the relatively balmy Gulf Stream climate, I later found that the Caddy family had set up a fertile garden and retreat following New Age principles – Christian-based but non-doctrinal with some almost mediumistic concepts.) She was over the moon in a spiritual sense. As her name was Sally, that of my oldest daughter, I listened up again. Another synchronicity. In Oban, I bought a sterling silver pendant and chain, a copy of the Celtic cross of St Martin that stands outside the little church of St David on the island of Iona. I still wear it around my neck to remind me of what I am not: not just a body but carrying a spirit with a purpose.

It is worth examining these facts in light of Gary Schwartz's book [3] to see how many 'coincidences' were involved. I asked my friend Anne (also the name of my daughter; coincidence 1) a question, knowing she was a Christian. She was also a professional primary school teacher, and she knew the simple answer (coincidence 2). I was nearly late for the church service and hesitated, and my guardian told me off (coincidence 3). My name was loudly called from the pulpit (coincidence 4). I was hailed by the girl from Mull, showing me the path that I must take (coincidence 5); her name was that of my oldest daughter (coincidence 6). Six 'events' qualify as Schwartz' Type III Synchronicity, or a supersynchronicity:

exceedingly improbable by chance yet occurring frequently for some people. It notably included a clairaudience, itself very persuasive.

These six striking experiences, crammed into one morning, changed my life and eventually that of my whole family. It was an epiphany, a spiritual experience with personal significance impossible to convey to others. They comprised meaningful coincidences that you can either choose to notice or sceptically dismiss as superstition. The circumstances of my invitation to Dunblane Cathedral meant that ignoring them was not an option. Is your glass half full? I realised that this is the basis of faith, namely trust. There are more ways to learn than by reason alone; this is Heart-knowing, but you should check it out by Mind-knowing too. That is the scientific method and the process I followed.

It was a journey that took several years. On my return to Canberra, I explored New Age and paranormal literature, always seeking to find hard facts. There was plenty of information available at that time but finding hard facts was trickier. I took a course in Transcendental Meditation (TM) and started meditating regularly, joined a local Findhorn group, went to a Canberra retreat run by Eileen Caddy, and attended the local Spiritualist Church. In February 1980, I attended an international transpersonal psychology meeting in Melbourne and was blown away by the emotional effect of group meditation with 400 experienced meditators. The robed Anglican priest who led the group wound up the session with, 'Hmm ... I bet there were some moist eyes after that.' Mine certainly were. My feelings were five seconds of utter bliss and a personal message: 'It's all okay, Peter; everything is all on track, all is as it should be.'

On 23 March 1980, I interviewed Les Danby in Melbourne following the publication of his book [4], an account of the mediumship of the modest carpenter Stan Walsh, mostly in the 20 years between World War I and World War II. He showed me Stan's 'Spirit Paintings' (pigments applied *through the glass)* and apports (objects materialised in trance), which I photographed. These are 'hard evidence', and I could not doubt his sincerity about how he came by them, although materialist science says that this is impossible. Six other witnesses, one a Justice of the Peace, verified his account. My only problem was that I did not see them happen: the account was second hand. While these accounts were strongly supportive of non-local mental action, I wanted hard, first-hand evidence. This gap was not filled for me until Saturday 23 May 1981, when I went through the following extraordinary experience.

Hard evidence. Knowing my interest in psychic phenomena, Mrs JS, the then president of the Canberra Spiritualist Society, asked me to witness 'psychic surgery' by a visiting Philippine practitioner. Mary and I arrived just before 6 pm. There was already a dozen or so mediums or friends of Mrs JS present, including Rev. JN and Mrs JN from Melbourne, the latter attending for treatment. Nestor (Nesta?), the psychic surgeon, was meditating. I was there regarding my sore eyes, then of seven months duration. Only a few of us (not Mary) were taken through; I was told to strip to my underpants and given a bathrobe. Several others were similarly robed, all female except Rev. JN. The following observations were taken from my notes made later that day, which I still have.

The only Asian person present was a slight young man wearing a very short-sleeved jacket or shirt without pockets over his trousers. Mrs JN was standing in her underpants with her back to me, and Nestor was holding a towel in front of her as though it were an X-ray machine. Her problem was very heavy menstrual flooding and lower abdomen pain, which she considered connected with her many babies. Nestor asked her to lie on the table and, without any preparation, immediately pushed both hands on her lower abdomen just above her underpants, pressing down quite hard with the tips of all eight fingers. After jiggling his hands up and down and wriggling his fingers sideways, his fingers were 1–2 inches *inside* her abdomen within three seconds. The entry area was making a loud succulent squishing noise as if he were rummaging around in the intestines. The wound was possibly three inches long – no more than the space occupied by his fingers – and was presenting about as much blood as I have seen with clean surgical incisions in which bleeding was controlled by clamps and sutures – not more than 5–10 ml. After 'rummaging' for perhaps 15–30 seconds, he withdrew his fingers, which were covered with blood, and his Australian assistant (a tall young man who had driven him from Sydney) carefully wiped the area clean with a sponge. There was nothing to be seen – no wound, no trace except a smear of blood and a faint red mark. Someone could have pushed their fingers 1–2 inches into the soft flesh of the lower abdomen, but, of course, there would be no break in the skin, no blood and no sound effects.

I watched all this from 3–4 feet away while Mrs JN was lying quietly. This was clearly observed by all six of us. There was no possibility of 'stage magic' (trick tubes, etc.), group hypnosis or other grounds for sceptical criticism. Nestor repeated this procedure twice elsewhere on her lower abdomen, then stood back, rinsed his hands in a bucket of water and dried them on a towel already holding some diluted bloodstains. Mrs JN got up, put her robe on and spoke to Nestor briefly; she was to repeat the treatment the next day.

(The following completes Mrs JN's history. About a year later, by extraordinary chance, I met Rev. JN on the street in Civic, Canberra – he lived in Melbourne, about 700 km away. He told me that the next day and in a subsequent treatment, Nestor removed 'handfuls' of sticky material from her abdomen and felt he had 'got it all'. Later that year, Mrs JN died from a massive, spreading gynaecological cancer.)

After Mrs JN, Mrs JS had a treatment on her neck. I was not told the problem, but I witnessed the same insertion of fingers, production of blood and sound effects. Then, to my surprise, it was my turn. Nestor spoke to me for the first time, and I saw that his eyes were unfocussed as if in an altered state of consciousness. He 'diagnosed' me with the towel and said he detected something in the bladder area as well as the eyes. I lay down on the table, and he repeated the abdominal procedure performed on Mrs JN but just above the pelvic bone. All I could feel was very strong pressure and kneading in that area, but by lifting my head, I could see that his fingers were up to at least the second joint *inside* my abdomen. The wound was again 2–3 inches long, and the space was filled with blood. There was considerable rummaging complete with sound effects, then he stood back, and the wound was tidied as before. But this time, some blood had spilled onto my underpants and soaked in. I still have these bloodstained underpants 40 years later (see Figure 1, taken February 2017); necessarily unwashed and being somewhat grisly evidence, I do not keep them in a display cabinet.

Nestor then announced he would look at my eyes. He told me to keep them shut at all times, then proceeded with a gentle massaging of my eyelids. I heard the squishing noises. When done, the area was wiped, and I was told to open my eyes. Everybody was looking at me with disbelief. Rev. JN said to me, 'As God is my witness, his fingers went up to the first joint *inside* your eyes and they were full of blood.' Since he was a pastor in a Christian church, I could not doubt him.

That was the first-hand evidence I needed. The lack of theoretical basis notwithstanding, I was sure that paranormal events could no longer be dismissed a priori. While not all such observations are genuine, I could no longer have any reason why they could not be so.

Prologue – The 'How' of this Book

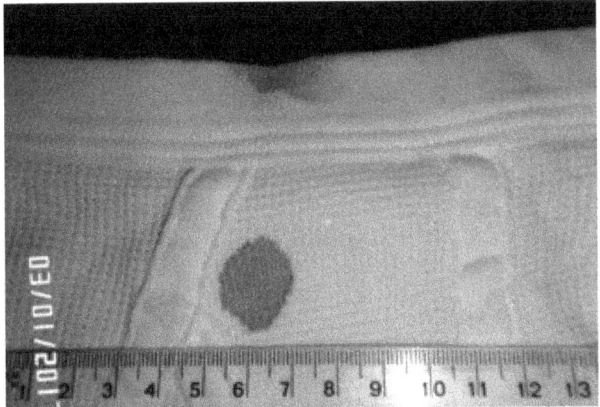

Figure 1. Bloodstains on Peter's underpants from 23 May 1981.

Conclusions:

- It was not a dream – it really happened as I remembered.
- See the book [5] on spiritual surgeons of the Philippines, which I picked up years later in an alternative bookshop. Some people have claimed the blood is a fake because it turned out to be chicken blood. I could have checked it, but I did not want to tamper with the evidence.
- In fact, the blood species is irrelevant – the issue was the materialisation of blood-like fluid where trickery was impossible.
- I give the surgeon top marks for diagnosis.
- I also give the surgeon top marks for psi effects, which could have a placebo improvement in some patients.
- There was no curative effect for me or for Mrs JN.

For the record, I had recently taken several megadoses of vitamin C as an experiment for a common cold. They had no effect on the cold but resulted in painful 'urinary gravel' that I identified chemically and microscopically as calcium oxalate, a rare breakdown product of ascorbic acid. Vitamin C is not necessarily harmless!

SUBSEQUENT YEARS

I, or sometimes my father (see instances 7 and 8), received many instances of psi happenings, events that could not be reasonably be explained by chance. Rather than detailing them, I will simply list them here:

1. two instances of remote viewing/location of desired objects
2. three instances of protection by a guardian angel/precognition of personal danger
3. one instance of synchronicity allowing a loving family telephone call
4. another veridical clairaudience
5. two instances of detailed precognitive dreams
6. two instances of extremely relevant sessions with a respected medium/clairvoyant
7. one very impressive deathbed experience from a beloved aunt
8. one out-of-body experience
9. three instances of explanatory experience after attending a church service
10. lifelong hindsight, including that I am a reincarnation of my maternal grandfather and my early career in microbiology showing him reasons for his early, painful death from appendicitis.

CONCLUDING THOUGHTS

All the observations in this section were just educational experiences. Since August 2020, I have resided in aged care in a southern suburb of the Australian Capital Territory, cradled by mountains of the beautiful Brindabella Ranges and within sight of the Namadgi National Park. It continues and extends my learning process as an exercise in sharing (see Chapter 7). Everybody in aged care lives with dementia, their own or other people's (see Chapter 1, Illusions of the First Kind – The Five Senses Determinant). They also live with the direct and humbling observation of other people's (sometimes huge) physical or mental burdens, how they do or do not cope and, for very few, the strengthening effect of religious faith.

Any significance of the old nursery rhyme (Thursday's Child has Far to Go) may simply reflect the fact that, in my 96th year I still haven't finished the book that you are reading.

REFERENCES

1. Beauregard M, Schwartz GE, Miller L, Dossey L, Moreira-Almeida, A, Schlitz, M, Sheldrake R, Charles Tart, C. (2014). Manifesto for a Post-Materialist Science. EXPLORE The Journal of Science and Healing 10(5): 272-274.
   https://doi.org/10.1016/j.explore.2014.06.008
2. Stevenson, I. (1997). *Where Reincarnation and Biology Intersect.* Praeger Publishers, Westport, CT.
3. Schwartz, G. E. (2017). *Super Synchronicity.* Param Media.
4. Danby, L.C. (1974). *The certainty of eternity as revealed by the mediumship of a Melbourne carpenter.* Hill of Content Publishing, Melbourne.
5. Whitescarver, J. (1976). *The truth behind the spiritual surgeons of the Philippines.* Awareness Research Center, Butler, NJ
6. Cooper, P.D. (2015). A Reverse-Paradigm Creed for the 21st Century: Why Many Scientists Still Have the Cart Before the Horse. *Explore.* 11(5):387-393.
7. Cooper, P.D. (2017). A Real Fifth Dimension? *Explore.* 13(1):62-67.
8. Cooper, P.D. (2018). Purpose: A Slow Dawning for Us All? *Explore.* 14(2), 144-148.
9. Cooper, P.D. (2018). Our great leap forward and us—right now. *Explore* 14(5), 305-308.
10. Cooper, P.D. (2019). The Importance of Sharing for Humanity and its Planet. *Explore* 15(5), 376-379.

Chapter 1
The Sacred, Magic Illusion that we live in

All the world's a stage and all the people merely players.
    Jacques, "As you like it"
        W. Shakespeare

Humanity lives within a precise set of illusions that are meant to serve humanity, but it must learn how to use them.
    "What God Said"
    Neale Donald Walsch

Universe of Maya - A Material Universe with Cryptic Meaning

SUMMARY

There was no beginning because time does not exist in reality. All that is and ever was is the One Mind and its Logos, its idea, its plan, its meaning. The One Mind knows itself by its reflection in its Logos. The material universe is a high-tech construct of the Logos. Science tells humanity that all that exists in the material universe comprises energy and consciousness, but humanity has no idea exactly what either means. This universe is considered a great, tripartite illusion: a stage-set whose purpose is sacred education through living a material animal (e.g., human) experience.

Any sufficiently advanced technology is indistinguishable from magic. (Arthur C. Clarke)

The rather plain but heavy lump of metal and plastic in my hand could have an alternate life as a chopping board in a very ordinary kitchen but, like Aladdin's lamp, if gently massaged in a special arcane way, images of my daughter's talented partner playing and singing his own compositions on YouTube appear. That, to me, is indistinguishable from magic. Somebody famous (who said it first is still being argued) went further, describing the universe as not only stranger than we think but also stranger than we can possibly imagine. In the near century since this was penned, the strangeness has simply got stranger [1,2].

Really highly advanced science is the same thing as spiritual understanding. The most important relationship is between each soul, an accumulation (or pattern?) of energy units, and God, the Source. This

Source is a subatomic force, the intelligent energy that fills and organizes all life. It is the beginning and the end, the Alpha and the Omega. It is the God of Creation.
And it is very much in Us. (Mayan of the Pleiades [3]).

ENERGY IS A BASIC FACT OF NATURE

What is energy? It is that which makes up all matter in the universe, is responsible for all its forces and phenomena, and fills all its space.

Energy self-assembles into tiny packets called subatomic particles, that is, statistical probabilities of energy node location. Those particles having mass comprise six types of quarks, six types of leptons (including the electron) and three types of bosons, while the gluon and the photon are massless. Gravity particles have not been detected.

Subatomic particles have the crucial property of being able to interact; we have no idea how. These interactions form what we know as matter. The interactions of matter come in four grades of strength:

- The weakest is gravity, an attractive force between all objects having mass over an infinite range, possibly via the zero-point field.
- Somewhat stronger, the weak force attracts quarks and leptons over a short range.
- Stronger still, the electromagnetic force acts on charged particles, repelling like charges and attracting opposites over an infinite range.
- Strongest, the strong force binds quarks together via the gluon over a short range.

By their intrinsic properties, subatomic particles can spontaneously combine to form protons, neutrons and simple atoms, mainly hydrogen, deuterium and helium. With extra energy, as in a supernova, all the atoms of the periodic table spontaneously arise, especially those essential for life. The importance of the exquisite balance of the intrinsic properties of these particles becomes obvious. But what is energy exactly? We do not know and do not even have a credible model.

CONSCIOUSNESS IS A BASIC FACT OF NATURE

What is consciousness? A much-debated topic, it is like information theory: a mix of hardware and software, engineering and message/meaning. But 'meaning' here seems to involve interpreting the context in terms of one's experiences – memories and innate and learned personality traits. An idea more in keeping with the Primal Mind is that Mind/consciousness is a pure, discarnate awareness defined as having the potential to know information, which then becomes a thought or idea. Mind is then a discarnate carrier of information. Where is all this activity happening? Some, possibly most, would say in a pattern of neural networks somehow derived and resident exclusively in the brain that has so far eluded mechanism or specific location; maybe it has no single place, like a hologram. Others would point out that there are aspects of information transfer that are independent of space-time, one of which was responsible for the quantum measurement problem; others propose that there is now overwhelming scientific evidence for a consciousness that is independent of space-time, previously arbitrarily dismissed; yet others who, from striking personal ('non-scientific') experiences, will know it to be so (derided by others lacking such experience). Regardless of the various perspectives, again, what is consciousness exactly? We do not know and do not even have a credible model. Possibly Mind and energy are different aspects of each other.

This is highly advanced technology.

TIME IS A BASIC FACT OF NATURE

What is time? Everybody knows what time is but, no better than St Augustine himself, modern philosophers or physicists still cannot define it. If you ask them what time is, the honest answer is probably 'we don't really know' [4]. Time, therefore, joins energy and consciousness as one of the foundational, vital mysteries.

Whether the material universe originated in a limited time (Big Bang) or in infinite time (a steady state [5]), it must be maintained by the balance between gravity (increasing order) and entropy (decreasing order). Gravity makes stars that liberate the energy that, in turn, allows planets to form and life to establish its niche. The process of the expenditure of this energy increases entropy and is responsible for time's irreversible arrow [6]. Both gravity and entropy depend on time.

We know that quantum waveforms are collapsed by conscious attention into subatomic particles that spontaneously assemble into material particles, as described later in this chapter. Such assembled matter then exists in a form that can absorb energy and will immediately do so. Thereafter, it is subject to the second law of thermodynamics and will enter the ebb and flow of entropy and gravity. Time is a necessary feature in this material universe where opportunity must be given for life to evolve in whatever niche it finds itself. If we live in a learning environment, as we explore below, one cannot learn without a progressively unfolding sequence of time, as provided by the flow of entropy. However, the original waveforms were in a quantum reality, where it is uncertain whether any sort of time exists.

Precognition and presentiment can unequivocally be demonstrated both experimentally and by psychic means [7,8,9,10,11]; there is ample evidence that they are exhibited in prophesy [12], dreams or by simple intuition. Perhaps Mind does not exist in material space-time in the first place [10]. The anomalies with time in our illusory universe may allow us a rare glimpse of the true underlying reality.

There is a sense in academia that events in time are 'spread out' somewhere, as on a map, which is accessible for 'reading' by an appropriately sensitive consciousness. It seems that the nature of time is fundamentally different in the two universes comprising the material universe (the kindergarten stage-set where we live) and the underlying reality. Time has been considered in both philosophy and physics under three headings: natural time, clock time and subjective time.

Natural time, or the nature of time. Natural time comprises the opposing philosophical viewpoints implied by Presentism v. Eternalism. Presentism says that time is no more than an ongoing series of 'now' moments, with any other time being moments that do not exist. Eternalism postulates that versions of the present are somehow laid out along the temporal dimension of the block universe in which we live. Buonomano [13] presents reasons why Einstein's special and general theories of relativity show strong arguments for preferring Eternalism. Eternalism is also strongly supported by the experimental evidence for precognition and presentience mentioned above.

Clock time. A clock is a machine or device that counts the number of oscillations of a calibrated periodic oscillator (a pendulum, a rotating wheel driven by a spring, a quartz crystal, a radioactive element) and translates the results into arbitrary time units (days, hours, minutes, seconds). It usually involves some form of entropy. However, clock time is not absolute; it is affected by gravity (as in global positioning system satellites) and by the clock's relative velocity, especially near light speed.

Subjective time. Subjective time refers to our conscious sense of time and is an illusion created by our brain, like our sense of colour; these are considered 'illusions of the first kind'. We are all familiar with an apparent flow of time; this may be more a contribution of memory, where successive 'now' moments are stitched together by short-term memory to create a mental movie with the appearance of flow. Neurones can be good oscillators but are poor at counting; subjective time is more important in detecting the momentary breaks ('subsecond timing') in speech and music that makes both intelligible than in measuring longer intervals, like waiting for traffic lights to change. Time appears absent in a near-death experience (NDE) [14], but Peake [15] suggests that perceived time is massively slowed in the nearly dying brain by floods of neurotransmitters, so the absence may be an artefact confined to the still-living brain.

ILLUSIONS OF THE FIRST KIND – THE FIVE SENSES DETERMINANT

It is hard to grasp the central conclusions of physics and chemistry that the material universe we live in is not really material at all. It is just designed to look that way. For example, science knows the eye to be no more than a self-maintaining camera, and the image on our retina is upside down; what we perceive visually is only an illusion inverted by the brain. In the same way, that oh-so-solid dining table is nothing more than a swirling mass of vibrating waveforms of pure energy that have been collapsed by some conscious attention into 'energies' that we call quarks, electrons etc., in an empty but busy space called the zero-point field. We can see the dining table because electromagnetic radiation physically bounces off (is reflected by) its organised bundle of energies. If it were not for the (probably non-) accident that we can only see in the very limited visible spectrum of light, say if we only had X-ray vision, we probably could not see the dining table at all. Our visual information is confirmed by our other senses for different physico-chemical reasons, so we have no reason to question our illusion. But the table as a table remains just an illusion, a brain-creation. There is no reason to believe that any material object differs

But there is much more to illusions of the first kind. In a remarkable series of books [16,17,18] occasional temporal lobe epileptic and migraineur Anthony Peake suggests a crucial aspect: these illusions are also there to protect our sanity from the effects of reality. As animals, humanity's primary job is to survive and thrive on the surface of planet Earth where we find ourselves. He uses a 'Huxleyan spectrum' (to honour Aldous Huxley) of related mental conditions – migraine, temporal lobe epilepsy, autism savants, schizophrenia, Alzheimer's disease – to illustrate the effect of an increasingly leaky 'reducing valve' exposing us to the progressively greater effect of reality, an incredibly busy field. As the father of a schizophrenic son, I understand his point. Aldous Huxley was one of the first to describe psychedelic drugs as 'opening the doors of perception' [19]. Peake continues by using the metaphor of the divided brain, well summarised by Iain McGilchrist (see Chapter 6), where the left brain is pictured as the struggling, ordinary, baser mind (the Eidolon) and the right brain as the continuing entity (the Daemon). It remembers all that soul's previous lives and the lessons learned (or not), based on the premise of reincarnation (see Chapter 4). The Daemon also remembers all events met; the inferences from these may be recalled as premonitions. It also has a degree of precognition. Peake suggests a healing role for the Daemon as 'the being in white' to soften the passage trauma of dying and supplying the life review (see Chapter 7) to educate in the process, filling the interval gained by slowing perceived time, as discussed previously. The Daemon can function as a guardian angel (see the next section) because it is part of the One Mind. Central to Peake's theme is that 'the brain acts as a receiver and its consciousness is located somewhere else'. (The musician is not inside the TV box). We go through life with one foot always in heaven, perhaps.

ILLUSIONS OF THE SECOND KIND – THE QUANTUM DETERMINANT

Is it not written in your law, I said, Ye are gods. (John 10:34)

Low-born clods
Of brute-earth
They aspire
To become gods,
Gods! Ha-Ha! (Chorus of Demons, 'The Dream of Gerontius', JH Newman)

A more subtle order of illusion has recently been brilliantly illuminated [20]. Many corollaries follow from Levy's book. This is a spiritual path; there is no objective reality; the present can reach backwards and forwards in time; all that is, is seamlessly interconnected in an immediate way; we all co-create our experiences; all things are in continuous flux, only patterns persist; everything that is, is a quantum thing, including the essential self; the universe is dream-like; the quantum determinant is neutral and can be used for good or evil. Our task is to recognise and choose to engage our quantum nature for the common good.

Simply put, Levy's proposal is no more than the quantum measurement problem, that is, conscious awareness determines a quantum outcome, or observing (giving attention to) a wave function is enough to collapse it into a particle. It was only considered a problem because it apparently violated realism, the notion that the universe really was as it seemed to the naive observer. This is well explained and validated elsewhere, notably Dean Radin and colleagues' brilliant proof of the role of consciousness in the collapse of the quantum wave function [21]. They used a double-slit optical system; this result was amplified in subsequent papers [22,23,24,25].

Carl Jung, who coined the term 'synchronicity' (a meaningful or immediately relevant coincidence) [26], noted a synchronicity in the astrological horoscopes of 483 married pairs compared with a control group comprising 32,200 unmarried pairs extracted from the same data. There was an expected significance in two 'aspects', one of which (conjunction of moon and moon) was highly significant by my chi-square calculation, with a probability of 10^{-7}, while the controls were $p > 0.15$, random values. The customary implication of planetary influences on people is difficult to maintain scientifically; the possibility of a cosmic hint of intention was not considered (i.e., some subtle plan at the pre-birth soul level [27]). One can see the plan if one looks in the right place.

Humans create their own dream as they go along, although, looking back on a long life, I personally believe the discarnate operator behaves more like one's personal guide or guardian that reflects the subconscious desires/needs of the individual. An element of trust is involved, and from my own lifetime, very likely an element of pre-planning.

Many books illustrate the guardian angel, some referenced in Brian Inglis's compelling *Coincidence: A Matter of Chance or Synchronicity?* [11], linked to the practice of sustained intention [28,29,30]. Church groups acknowledge healing by group prayer, supported by experiment, especially if led by a skilled healer in 'cordial' environments [31]. We know from experiments that mental constructs can be transferred to other non-local minds, and groups can amplify the effect [10]. We also know that the concentration of many minds on one large event can persuade random number generators into less random (coherent) behaviour [10]. Deliberate group Peace TM has given many signs that community violence can be lessened locally [32], and group online peace meditation can promote group reactions akin to religious experiences [30].

The independence from time is prominent. The effect is generally benevolent, any apparently joking effect seemingly with a teaching intent.

This gnosis is revealingly like that described for the Dreaming of the First Nations Australians (see Chapter 7). It suggests that one crucial future advance may be the ability to communicate non-verbally (telepathically), rendering deception, literally, unthinkable.

Some other conclusions may be summed up in Knox's quasi-schoolboy and very English limericks (see Chapter 2), the second of which may be worth repeating here:

Dear Sir, your astonishment's odd.
I am always about in the Quad.
And that's why the tree
Will continue to be,
Since observed by, Yours faithfully, God.

ILLUSIONS OF THE THIRD KIND – THE CURRICULUM DETERMINANT

The illusions reported by Neil Donald Walsch [33] (quoted in the Prologue to this Chapter), as part of his messages received by automatic writing, are of a different order again. The 10 illusions are listed as perceived problems of daily living, the seeming wave-slaps (some overwhelmingly monstrous but never lethal to the soul) in the face of the long-distance swimmer that, in fact, do not exist. They are listed as need, failure, disunity, insufficiency, requirement, judgement, condemnation, conditionality, superiority and ignorance. These all follow from the proposition that there is only One Thing, and all things are part of the One Thing. All we need to do is share and help each other; kindness is key. There is no such thing as right and wrong, only what works and what does not work; this simply restates the laws of karma.

The core of this quotation is the injunction that humans must learn how to use the illusions (see Chapter 6). They are no more than teaching tools; to quote Joan Baez's song 'God is God' and a familiar New Age concept, 'just another lesson'. Not easy, just non-negotiable. Hence the concept of the kindergarten. Love is all that is.

THE PARTY LINE FROM SCIENCE ON THE ORIGIN OF THE UNIVERSE – ANOTHER ILLUSION?

Current ideas of the origin of the universe have gelled firmly around a Big Bang (standard cosmology [SC]) rather than some steady state (infinite time) variant. Despite that, the SC is unsafe because of many problems, and each claimed support for the SC has a feasible alternative. In addition, structures called supercluster complexes [34] – huge groupings of galaxies – by themselves rule out an origin as recent as 13.8 billion years ago, as they would have taken about 60 billion years to form. Accordingly, we have explored [5] a novel steady state universe, a relation between entropy and gravity that drives the maintenance and growth of the universe (see Figure 2).

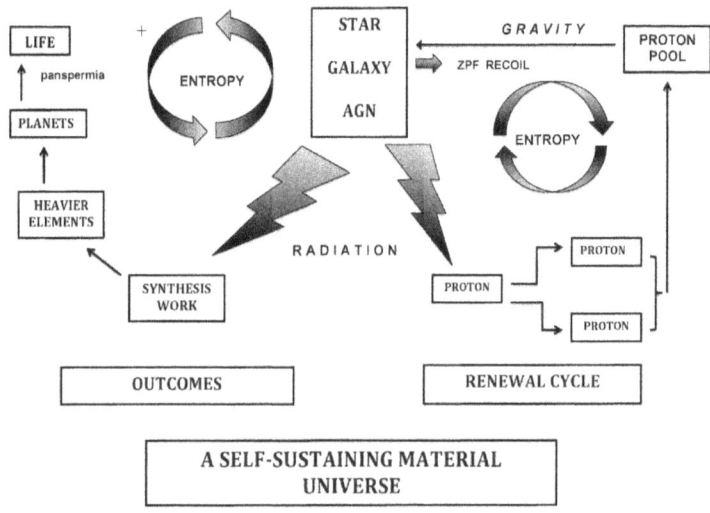

Figure 2. Diagram of a feasible self-sustaining material universe. This model requires three testable postulates, as explained in the text quoted.
Abbreviations: AGN, active galactic nucleus; ZPF, the zero point field.

The material universe stands revealed as a well-oiled perpetual motion machine, endlessly recycling energy that is ultimately derived from the quantum vacuum virtual plasma of infinite space and infinite time. The choice is between a universe that has a beginning and, therefore, an end (Big Bang), and a universe that has always been and always will be (steady state).

DISCUSSION

What are we to make of all this make-believe? We may have a momentary problem because we are being obliged to live through a lie. Then one sees that this was no more an untruth than is a stage play, 'All the world's a stage and all the people merely players'. We just have to work this out for ourselves: the realisation that we exist in a kindergarten stage-set is part of our free-choice education. This concept is discussed in Chapter 5 and is what the Messengers were trying to tell us (see Chapter 2). Thus, we inhabit a material realm that is delicately crafted to defy reality, a magic universe of Mind-stuff.

Since it does not seem to affect activities of daily living, humanity is no more obliged to 'make anything of it' than are the birds and the bees. After it evolved into the genus *Homo*, humanity also did not, for perhaps one or two million years. Then something changed: humanity achieved what amounted to a breakthrough (see Chapter 5).

Human culture made its great leap forward: a 'quantum advance in human ability to innovate that marks the dawn of human culture'. One archaeological marker of this was the use of the bright-red mineral red ochre (iron oxide), of no obvious use to hunter-gatherers but nevertheless mined, traded and carried long distances and used at specific sites in East Africa; it is still regarded as sacred by First Nations Australians and used in closed initiation ceremonies. Another marker was the abrupt transition into the Upper Palaeolithic some 200,000–400,000 years ago, a sudden improvement in stone tool technology.

Historians have not decided what the impetus was. My personal preference (see Chapter 5) was to ascribe this to the kind of insights that are found by those undergoing a NDE [14], where certain individuals pass through a crisis that transforms their lives and often confers psychic abilities that register as shamanism. It was the dramatic and shocking awareness of a spiritual dimension, including the supernatural, and the exercise of creative imagination.

These abilities and the change in attitudes must have had an equally dramatic effect on the tribe, especially in the likely event of an esteemed elder as the central character. The inference was that access to a Universal Mind would increase ideation, leading to increased innovation.

We considered the quantum determinant as a crucial factor in the unfolding role of humanity. Here we are indebted to the healer and Tibetan Buddhist practitioner Paul Levy [20] for his insights. His autobiographical notes show degrees in economics and studio art, an interesting blend of rationalist and intuitive and a keen interest in quantum physics – the field where both personality types are at home. In his mid-twenties, he passed through bipolar-psychotic experiences intriguingly resembling NDEs, resulting in a mystical awakening/shamanic initiation, which he continued to develop.

The worldwide nature of the great leap awareness is illustrated by the myth of the boatman of the dead, the ferryman and the river, a likely result of an NDE. A Westerner would at once recognise Charon and the Styx; an Ancient Egyptian would recognise Aken and his ferryman Mahaf, and a First Nations Australian would see Wuluwait, the boatman of the dead bound for Purelko, the afterlife. While the European culture may be derived from the Egyptian culture, their huge dispersion in space and time from the Australian culture suggests an independent origin. Indications that other independent, ancient cultures share this myth are found in the Native American and shamanic literature.

But is there a deeper significance to all this, and does the universe have a purpose? Living things show a clear purpose and exert a huge effort to maintain themselves and their ecosystem in a variable environment, even to the extent of self-extinction to preserve progeny. In the special case of humanity, the 'why' question is not widely asked of any purpose once a critical phase of childhood is passed. In time, most humans see their own mortality and wonder if 'that is all there is' and 'what is the point of it all'. Is there a point? (see Chapter 4).

Over millennia, many humans with the character of Messengers (see Chapter 2) have appeared with a unanimous message for those who ask this question: 'you are not a human being in search of a spiritual experience; you are a spiritual being immersed in a human experience'.

This completely changes the story. The relevance of the Shakespearean quotation (see the Prologue to this Chapter) immediately reveals a point to the brilliant and beautiful illusion in which we live. Of course, we are not obliged to accept that we are here to learn lessons unless we wish to; we have free choice as to where we do or do not place our trust. I hope my personal preference is obvious.

CONCLUSIONS

Some great Mind has created a realistic stage-set for the play of life, for uncountable billions of planets universe-wide. The building blocks were energy and consciousness, shaped into entities whose intrinsic properties were exactly right for spontaneous assembly into the material universe that we observe. Despite humanity's current consensus that our universe is slowly dying, it makes more sense to me that it is everlasting, and evidence is quoted to support that.

Once we understand that we are merely actors in the great play, we have the motivation to understand the purpose that this incredibly beautiful kindergarten has prepared for us. For humanity now, it must include planetary healing. Progress was not meant to be easy, just non-negotiable.

REFERENCES

1. Talbot M. *The Holographic Universe*. HarperCollins Australia;1996.
2. Lewels J. *The God Hypothesis: Extraterrestrial Life and its Implications for Science and Religion.* 2nd Ed. Granite Publishing, Columbus, NC; 2005.
3. Maclaine, S. *Out on a Limb*. Bantam Books, NY; 1983.
4. Riggs P. (2020). 'Physics, Philosophy and the Nature of Time': ABC interview, P. Adams https://www.abc.net.au/radionational/programs/latenightlive/timepeter-riggs/11963494
5. Cooper PD. A Steady State Better Explains a Metrically Expanding Universe and the Vital Interplay of Entropy and Gravity. *Intl J Astrobiology Aerospace Technol* 02:107; httpps://gavinpublishers.com/assets/articles_pdf/1570626126article_pdf18065791.pdf
6. Rovelli C. *The Order of Time*. Allen Lane, Penguin Random House, UK; 2018.
7. Le Shan L. *A New Science of the Paranormal: The Promise of Psychical Research*. Quest Books. Wheaton IL; 2009.
8. Tart CT. *The End of Materialism*. Oakland CA, Petaluma CA: New Harbinger Publishers. Institute of Noetic Sciences;2009.
9. McLuhan R. *Randi's Prize: What Sceptics Say About the Paranormal, Why They Are Wrong and Why It Matters*. Matador Troubador Leicester, UK; 2010.
10. Radin D. *Supernormal. Science, Yoga, and the Evidence for Extraordinary Psychic Abilities*. New York: Crown Publishing Group; 2013.
11. Inglis B. *Coincidence: A Matter of Chance- or Synchronicity?* Guildford, UK. White Crow Books Ltd; 2012.
12. Osborn AW. *The Future is Now*. Quest Book Edition, The Theosophical Publishing House, Wheaton, IL;1967.
13. Buonomano, D. *Your Brain is a Time Machine; the Neuroscience and Physics of Time*. W.W. Norton & Co. Inc. New York, NY;2017.
14. Ring K. *Lessons from the Light: What we can learn from the Near-Death Experience*. Moment Point Press, Needham, MA; 2006.
15. Peake A. *The Daemon: A Guide to Your Extraordinary Secret Self.* Arcturus Publishing Ltd, London UK; 2011.

16. Peake A, *Is There Life After Death? The Extraordinary Science of What Happens When We Die*. Arcturus, London;2006.
17. Peake A. *Opening the Doors of Perception: The Key to Cosmic Awareness*. Watkins Media Ltd. Kindle Edition; 2016.
18. Peake A. *The Infinite Mindfield: A Quest to Find the Gateway to Higher Consciousness*. Watkins Publishing Ltd. London UK; 2013.
19. Huxley, A. *The Doors of Perception*. Random House, London UK; 1954. 2019.
20. Levy P. *The Quantum Revelation: A Radical Synthesis of Science and Spirituality*. New York SelectBooks Inc.; 2018.
21. Radin D, Michel L, Galdamez K, Wendland P, Rickenbach R, Delorme A. (2012). Consciousness and the double-slit interference pattern: Six experiments. *Physics Essays. 2012;* 25(2) 157- 171. doi: 10.4006/0836-1398-26.4.553
22. Radin D, Michel L, Johnston J, Delorme, A. (2013). Psychophysical interactions with an double-slit interference pattern. *Phys. Essays* 26, 553–566.
23. Radin D, Michel L, Pierce A, Delorme, A. (2015). Psycho-physical interactions with a single-photon double-slit optical system. *Quantum Biosys.* 6, 82–98.
24. Radin D, Michel L, Delorme, A. (2016). Psychophysical modulation of fringe visibility in a distant double-slit optical system. *Phys. Essays* 29, 14–22.
25. Radin D, Wahbeh H, Michel L, Delorme A. (2020). Commentary: False positive effect in advanced meta-experimental protocol. Frontiers in Psychology 11, 726-728
26. Jung CG. *Synchronicity: an acausal Connecting Principle*. London UK: Routledge; 1955. 36.
27. Schwartz, R. 2009. *Your Soul's Plan: Discovering the Real Meaning of the Life You Planned Before You Were Born*. North Atlantic Books, Berkeley CA.
28. Anon. *It Works. The Famous Little Red Book That Makes Your Dreams Come True*. De Vorss & Co, Publisher, Camarillo, CA; 1926; 1953.
29. McTaggart L. *The Intention Experiment: Use Your Thoughts to Change the World*. HarperCollins Publishers, London, UK; 2007.
30. McTaggart L. *The Power of Eight: Harnessing the Miraculous Energies of a Small Group to Heal Others, Your Life and the World*. London UK: Hay House; 2017.
31. Dossey L. Healing Research: What we Know and Don't Know. *Explore.* 2008; 4(6):34-35.

32. Old J. *The Super Radiance Effect: A Proven Technology for National Invincibility and International Peace*. Wimborne St Giles, Dorset: Team Business Development Ltd; 2017
33. Walsch ND. *What God Said: The 25 Core Messages of Conversations with God That Will Change Your Life and the World*. London: Hodder and Stoughton; 2013.
34. Lerner, EJ. *The Big Bang Never Happened. Amazon Australia Services Inc. Vintage Edition;* 2012

Chapter 2
Many Messengers, One Message

*"You are not a human being in search of a spiritual experience.
You are a spiritual being immersed in a human experience."*

A Reverse-Paradigm Creed for the Twenty-First Century: Why Many Scientists Still Have the Cart Before the Horse

Science, religion and philosophy should ultimately come together like the meridians at the pole.
Attributed to Pierre Theilhard de Chardin, SJ.

SUMMARY

All that is, and ever was, is the One Mind, and the material universe is considered a great illusion, as shown in Chapter 1.

Over the last 10,000 years of human history, many Messengers have come with the unanimous message: 'you are not a human being in search of a spiritual experience; you are a spiritual being immersed in a human experience'.

If they have any intrinsic value, then science, religion and philosophy should ultimately come together like the meridians at the pole. In fact, they do, in the most profound aspects of both: quantum mechanics and meditative absorption, respectively. The essential unity of everything becomes clear – all is part of one and vice versa. The meeting point is the Primal Mind. The universe looks more like a great thought than a great machine.

The idea that the Mind came first is as old as humankind's creation myths, but science usually sets it aside the better to study nature's machinery. Brain-first seems to have cemented nowadays as the only acceptable scientific worldview. Lester Smith reintroduced Mind-first in 1975 [1], more elegantly than here and with much more scholarship, gently reminding us that the 'common-sense' brain-causes-consciousness paradigm was only a working hypothesis to test itself and had so far failed validation. He pointed out that quantum mechanics (QM) taught us to beware of such common sense and that the Mind-first paradigm solved many puzzles in cosmology and theoretical physics without bending nature's laws, incidentally blending with the intuitions of most of humankind and, notably, the worldview highly refined by quantum theory pioneers [2,3.] Forty years on, Brain-first validation is still lacking, and two remarkable, contrary scientific facts have become thoroughly firm (psi phenomena and the quantum measurement problem). These have been hitherto deliberately dismissed as impossible and beyond science, hardly a scientific choice. As in 1975, humanity's problems and attitudes still stem from a mistaken world paradigm, and its sensible retake is even more urgent.

Fr Pierre's insight suggests a walkable pathway to review this mistake, with our imaginary Walker an unversed, naive but very rational and intelligent student walking it for the first time.

IS THERE A RELEVANT, SIMPLE MESSAGE FROM SCIENCE?

Our Walker sees in the panoply of science a scintillating array of information jewels as awe-inspiring as the desert sky at night but more orderly and a fraction of that which is not seen. Among them, the Walker chooses the following as bearing directly on our illusion: they are enlarged upon in Chapter 3.

The observer effect and the wave–particle duality of light. Apparent wave–particle duality is the defining characteristic of small particles (electrons, atoms, molecules, photons). The act of *gaining information* about their normally wave-like state seems to abruptly contract or collapse them to a particle-like state (see Chapter 1). However, the maths of information theory now suggests a conceptual basis for QM that reveals basic particles, such as electrons, to be bits or packets of information [4]. The history of the universe is a story of increasing information content, and perhaps information per se is the ultimate reality. However, we have no concept for pure information except in relation to a carrier, say computer code or letters on a page: it is meaningless until read out. Nevertheless, information as an idea in the mind is real enough. Thus, information has the *potential* to be known, depending on how it is observed, but 'knowing' demands the presence of a consciousness or mind. Only then does it become an idea or thought. In fact, it seems difficult to separate mind and matter at quantum levels.

But this led to another paradox, familiarly penned against an unrelated philosophical principle [5]:

> There was a young man who said 'God
> Must find it exceedingly odd
> To think that the tree
> Should continue to be
> When there's no-one about in the Quad'.

More on this later.

The Finely Tuned Universe

Where (at least) six fundamental constants have all to be within very exact limits to allow galaxies, planets and carbon atoms to form (see Chapter 3).

Paranormal (Psychic) Phenomena

For 100 years, paranormal phenomena have been considered outside the bounds of real science, a kind of pseudoscience relegated to the province of fools [6]. However, many reasonable persons have experienced them, religious or not, more stunningly persuasive than the strange coincidences of Jungian synchronicity (see Chapter 1); this concept is explored in Chapters 3 and 4. Their very mention may turn some readers off at this point; our Walker, innocent of prior ideologies, has the intellectual curiosity to continue. The Walker stands aghast at the prejudiced derision of the sceptics but recognise that, thanks to the sceptics' steadfast faith and intransigent criticisms, the methodology of psychical research has improved to the extent that reasoned grounds for objection can no longer be found. Several excellent, modern summaries of more than a century of such research detail massive amounts of corroborating data (see Chapter 1) and the important role of the die-hard sceptic (see Chapter 4). It is now unscientific, even irresponsible, to continue to ignore them.

The Walker observes that life did indeed develop on one suitable planet (Earth). The odds against suitability were high – not only in the narrow habitable zone of the central star to allow liquid water but also in that there was enough mass to retain that water, enough iron to form a magnetic field protective against ionising radiation, enough carbon dioxide to precipitate the dissolved iron from that water, enough other elements to grow a diverse primordial soup and enough photosynthesis to convert almost all of that carbon dioxide into oxygen to allow an ozone layer to protect the land surface from non-ionising radiation (UV) and permit oxygen-breathing life. This process has also been remarkably fast: after the hypothesised Big Bang, the first stars were of hydrogen, making mainly helium; only secondary and large, very hot stars can explode to make heavier atoms from helium. Earth's star is a cool tertiary formed from the debris of a secondary star. An average star life is about 10 billion years; Earth's star is almost half done (4.5 billion years).

Life on Earth also developed very quickly – half a billion years to solidify, half a billion to form oceans. Primitive life (stromatolite) was already found. It took a further three billion years to develop multicellular life, and only a half-billion more years to the present huge biodiversity. The Walker found that many scientists think that life formed by chance also, much as a billion monkeys on a billion typewriters, given enough time, could eventually produce all the sonnets of Shakespeare. However, the Walker noticed that, with some 40 keys on the QWERTY keyboard and some 40 letters/spaces per sonnet line, it would take 40^{40} tries to get only one of the 14 lines of one of the 154 sonnets right. Since the solar system is $< 10^{18}$ seconds old (according to the Standard Cosmology), there has not really been enough time for monkeys: somebody wrote the sonnets. Similar reasoning could apply to the simple protein human proinsulin, with 86 amino acids and a pool of 40 candidates (D and L amino acid isomers in the primordial soup). However, proteins do not generally arise de novo and cannot be thought of this way. One must examine their genes. Fortunately, Dawkins [6] reminded the Walker of the cogent power of Darwinian selection to speed-up random processes, producing this power as if explaining the rapidity of spontaneous life creation and evolution.

But Dawkins left it there and failed to follow up with the maths. Darwinian selection needs random mutations in DNA to select from, and these occur at about one per site per 10^7 generations. To work through the 258 base pairs of, for example, the proinsulin gene at random would take $\sim 3 \times 10^9$ generations, say only ~90,000 years for modern microbes and 60 times longer for mammalian cells. However, this would produce $2^{1,000,000,000}$ progenies, a number again beyond astronomical sizes. Darwinian selection would need to occur very often, but the selection criteria are unclear for proinsulin (ignoring the need for its further processing and for specific and matching cell adaptations). Some purposeful direction seems involved. For example, a *perceived need* for a light-sensitive skin patch to avoid predators could guide a creative Mind to evolve an eye. The Walker realises that such speculation rapidly becomes specious and daunting when applied to, for example, the complex gene steps required in evolving a vertebrate eye, which Dawkins dismisses with his 'half an eye' concept. This does not even approach the entire gene pool on Earth and serves only to show how hard it is to propose the purely random generation of life, given the time constraints. Apparently, arguments like these changed the mind of the once-atheist philosopher Anthony Flew [7]. Having accepted the overwhelming evidence for the deliberate creation of a life-friendly universe, the Walker sees no rational objection to deliberate creation of life and can only accept it as the least unlikely idea.

IS THERE A RELEVANT, SIMPLE MESSAGE FROM RELIGION?

Our Walker, on confronting the massif of religion, discovers a plethora of words. The Walker rejects the non-rational issue of faith as an acceptance of given truth without corroborative evidence but acknowledge its value in the survival of scholarship and faith itself through the dark Middle Ages. An abstract consciousness or Primal Mind is generally central, but a specific name is preferred, God in various languages who may assume different personalities.

It is disappointing to see organised religion confused with spiritual awareness. Religion is no more than our attempt to organise spiritual awareness into formal associations. The history of religion is as sordid as any political process; the professed atheist Richard Dawkins rightly chastised Christianity over examples such as the Crusades and the Inquisition. Yes, the bathwater of Christianity stinks but, like it or not, there is a baby in it. That baby is spiritual awareness.

In contrast, the history of spiritual awareness is remarkable and uplifting. Its essence can be found in two ancient insights: reincarnation and the NDE (see Chapters 4 and 7). 'I do not hold with such fairy tales,' you may retort, and that is your loss: many convincing studies and books are now available (see Chapter 1). Reincarnation was accepted as obvious in the time of Jesus and in traditional societies, including among First Nations Australians, as well as everywhere outside the Christian–Islamic sphere. But reincarnation was banned in Western churches for political reasons (see Chapter 4).

Atheism

The Walker meets a vociferous band denying that a Primal Mind or God can exist, usually also denying any validity in supportive evidence. Some claim a Primal Mind is unnecessary or wildly improbable, it being simpler to assume nothing, but this belies the overwhelming non-simplicity of nature. Many self-styled atheists cannot say they believe that God does not exist, only that they do not believe God exists; such a neutral stance hardly differs from agnosticism. Atheists puzzle the Walker given the foregoing data from science, particularly as many of them are scientists. The sincere Christianity of the greatest explainers of acts of God – Newton and Darwin – thus seems a paradox. Perhaps science remembers the treatment of Galileo and the consistent obstructionism of the act of God concept ('God of the Gaps'), routinely explaining any then-inexplicable aspect of science. Such blocks continue, especially in the form of creationist theory, for example. The Walker notes that no scientist, mindful of his grant source, mentions God in his papers.

Nevertheless, the scientist must try hard to avoid the act of God explanation lest they miss a real one; this has been the great gift of the enlightenment to our understanding of nature. It follows that any Primal Mind interpretation may need overwhelming statistical odds but not that it is unthinkable; even then, some sceptics persist as an act of faith (see Chapter 4).

In his enjoyable but very one-sided *The God Delusion*, Dawkins [6] rails against the God hypothesis, but he is less than honest. No actual evidence against this idea is given except its high improbability, whereas the real improbability is the existence of life itself. He is really criticising organised religion, mainly Christianity, played out through the tribal viciousness of human nature. Perhaps *The Religion Delusion* was not a very catchy title. The Primal Mind concept is little considered. The disgusting and barbaric bits in the Old Testament, the often-unattractive aspects of Jehovah and the emphasis on fear, not love, are all noted. The timely message of peace and love from Jesus of Nazareth is muddied by the bloodthirstiness of the age, superstition and the equally vile language in, for example, Revelations. He almost does not need to point out the more than two millennia of atrocities that continue in religion's name. Dawkins is only partly right: the unsavoury bathwater of organised religion does not affect the baby in it.

The almost universal human yearning for a God figure is ascribed to childhood gullibility where trust in authority has survival value [6], but it could equally derive from ancestral memories: humans may recall both origins and intervals between incarnations (see Chapter 4).

Christianity

The most numerically supported religion, Christianity relies on its Holy Scripture, the Bible; the Old Testament also underlies the smaller numbers of Judaism. The Walker notes this as transcribed oral history of a preliterate nomadic desert tribe in a brutal world, with origin myths familiar in such societies. Moses's Ten Commandments provide specific instructions – six for peaceful group living while first always enjoining non-material monotheism with respect and thoughtfulness of that single Mind-like deity. Another constant was that the Mind came first, then it created the world. The New Testament rests on the message of Jesus of Nazareth, a revolutionary novelty for a bloodthirsty age in the West, that of universal peace, kindness, respect and perhaps brotherly love, even outside the family or tribe. Pope Gregory (The Great) and St Thomas Aquinas listed seven cardinal sins and their corresponding virtues: pride v. humility; greed v. sharing; envy v. gratitude; gluttony and drunkenness v. temperance; anger v. patience;

sloth v. conscientiousness. Their equivalents can mostly be found in the laws of karma, which are also mirrored in the New Testament ('what you sow is what you reap', Galatians 6:7; Matthew 7:1; Matthew 7:12); the Golden Rule ('Do as you would be done by') restates The First Great Law of Karma. Alone among the Messengers, the later deification of Jesus parallels thinking in Ancient Rome, several emperors were deified too.

Islam

The second-largest religion in numbers, Islam is a direct descendant of both Judaism and Christianity. Here the Walker finds a clear directive: 'there is no entity deserving of worship but God, and Mohammed is his Messenger'. Moses, Abraham and Jesus are also accepted as Messengers, mystics with special intuitive insights perhaps acquired during meditation. The Messengers were sent to instruct humankind how God wishes it to live, particularly the constant mindfulness of God, charity to humankind and self-denial. Again, Mind came first. The sacred scripture the Qur'an also embodies the essentials of Christianity.

Hinduism

The oldest and third-largest religion, Hinduism has no single founder, scripture nor commonly agreed creed and could be defined by what most Hindus believe. Hindus (mostly) believe in a supreme God or Mind, with various aspects or attributes being represented by nominal deities. Particularly appealing to the Walker is Shiva the Nataraj, Lord of the Dance, where the entire universe can be viewed as a performance with humankind playing the role of audience and performer, the dance stands with or without an audience. Life is a cycle of birth, death and rebirth governed by karma or how previous lives were lived; the 12 Laws of Karma all follow from The Great Law of Cause and Effect that one reaps what one sows: what a person puts out in life is what they receive from life. Christianity and Buddhism say the same. The main sacred literature comprises the Vedas ('knowledge'), discussing dharma, or code of conduct, law, duty, virtue and morality. Centrally, the atman (spiritual being) has a human experience rather than a human having a spiritual experience. Mind came first.

Buddhism

In contrast, Buddhists strive for a deep insight into the true nature of life but postulate no deity, focusing on personal spiritual development involving morality, meditation and wisdom. The Messenger was Prince Gautama, the Buddha (Enlightened One, ca 500 BC).

In a highly memorable video, the Dalai Lama once declared, 'my religion is kindness'. And that was it. Nothing more, despite an immense body of literature. One recoils at the size of a similar declaration by an archbishop, imam, rabbi, swami or guru.

The core difference is that Buddhism does not require belief, except perhaps that 'what goes around, comes around': life can be observed to be like that (karma). The Buddha knew that people have difficulty believing something they cannot see, touch, taste, hear or smell, and what was experienced by some charismatic prophet centuries ago – no matter how vivid or with whatever miracles – may not be convincing to those who come later. Discourse on a deity is discouraged, concentrating on personal responsibility and right behaviour for their own sake, with the clear understanding of repeated reincarnation for however long it takes to get the lessons right.

If you think that kindness is somehow not strong, not masculine, somehow flabby or weak-kneed, think again. Or rather try it for yourself; it is, in fact, damnably hard. If you cannot love your fellow man, it is not dishonest to act always as if you do – with kindness.

Reincarnation is central; with successive lives comes a progressive freeing from earthly desires. A core text comprises the Sutras of Patanjali [8], 196 aphorisms referring to meditative absorption, the practice of yoga, the extraordinary abilities (siddhis) sometimes incidentally met and personal happiness and liberation. The yogic path is mastering the skills of dispassion and deep meditation, a physical and mental exercise to separate oneself from thoughts and feelings. One aims to simply be, not think, not judge, just be focused and aware – at peace. Meditation is part of virtually all religious practice, although not often under that name. Much evidence indicates that meditation, religious or not, can benefit health and happiness.

The true heart of Buddhism is the Law of Dependent Co-arising, the non-local, entangling, fundamental process that gives shape to material existence [9]. There is no functional difference between this concept and what is taken as 'God' in most peoples' minds, except perhaps the realisation that we are also part of this divinity. If you 'talk to God', you are also talking to all minds that have ever existed, since all have become One Mind, with the infinite wisdom that implies. We are all quantum entities, not separate but interdependent, interrelated, co-arising together, infinitely connected to the whole universe but free, like photons in a beam of light. Buddhism anticipates QM (Chapter 1, Illusions of the Second Kind – The Quantum Determinant).

While Buddhism has no deity, it may not need one as its total focus on the mind conforms to general religious concepts and practice. Significantly, paranormal phenomena that are difficult for Westerners to accept are commonplace to Easterners as the siddhis of experienced meditators [8], who incidentally perform better in paranormal tests than untrained subjects. There are several mentions of 'higher, divine or celestial beings' in the sutras (i.e., a spiritual hierarchy). Conceivably any improvement in the individual mind by personal happiness or liberation can ipso facto improve the aggregate Mind.

Newer Aspects

Jesus's, Mohammed's and the yogis' healing and other powers were compelling to their contemporaries; parallel but rare stories of similar (psychic or siddhi) powers are found in recent times [10,11] (and in the first section of this book). In particular, Sri Satya Sai Baba [12,13] was a modern Messenger embracing Hinduism (his own) but also Buddhism, Christianity, Islam and Zoroastrianism (Parsi), with a large following in India and worldwide, divine connotations and well-attested siddhis. His central message is the constant one: that humankind is a spiritual being temporarily tied to a material body, needing to free itself from earthly desires to avoid continually returning to Earth. One must avoid evil, serve others and be constantly mindful of the divine. Sai Baba passed away in 2011, leaving an immense legacy of charitable and educational service to India and the world. A recent testimony to his gifts is a book by the Icelandic psychologist Professor Erlendur Haraldsson [14], also noted for his parapsychological investigations. Haraldsson spent much time in India, had many interviews with Sai Baba, witnessed many manifestations of objects and interviewed dozens of witnesses of materialisations. Sai Baba consistently declined scientifically controlled investigations. Examples of unexplained healings abound, inadequately documented in Haraldsson's opinion. Sai Baba affected the lives of millions of people, in new ideals or renewing old ones. 'Love all, serve all'.

IS THERE A RELEVANT, SIMPLE MESSAGE FROM PHILOSOPHY?

The Walker sees the foregoing as legitimately also within the ancient province of philosophy. The basic position of science itself pre-empts many questions in epistemology, with its prime emphasis on observation with which reason must also tally exactly. Both must ideally be quantitated, with added experimentation wherein parameters are measured under systematically varied conditions. Logic, especially the definitive logic of mathematics, is vital but, along with most scientific data, has advanced far beyond that of the ancients. Ordinary, 'common-sense' observation suffices for classical (Newtonian) macrophysics, but a new type of thinking was needed for subatomic dimensions. Here, the manner of knowing affects the outcome, and epistemology and ontology became part of the deductive process; a wave–particle complementary duality became the defining paradigm. This is analogous to a Mind–energy (matter) duality, possibly also complementary, implied by aspects of paranormal phenomena. The implications of quantum theory go to the heart of metaphysics, and the three scientific choices above to that of cosmology and ontology. Many scientists cannot contemplate science without also straying into aesthetics, while others are not bothered by that distraction.

Ethics or moral philosophy seems in a special position. The scientist is wedded to objective truth and is wary of self-deception or speculation except as a basis for practical experimentation, but truth in religion is subjective. A universal emphasis in religion is on good rather than evil, right rather than wrong. At first, the Walker is not concerned about absolute standards as, usually, it is clearly relative: what is right for the tiger can be decidedly wrong for the gazelle. All major religions insist on rules of behaviour that are incidentally necessary for a harmonious and prosperous human society reconciling tribal differences, especially as its size approaches the sustainable limit of the planet. Thus the primary religious emphasis is right if not essential for the human species, although that species is slow to recognise it. The hard-wired instincts enabling human dominance in the jungle of Darwinian selection may have to be consciously overridden. There are signs that this is slowly happening (in places) – no public executions, then no judicial murder at all; no slavery; seeing the folly of war and what causes it (within Europe anyway); the horror of nuclear and chemical weapons (after bitter lessons); universal suffrage; and the sexual revolution with manageable birth-rates – and the key may be universal high literacy and communication.

Another consistent feature is the repeated emergence of Messengers, charismatic personalities often with paranormal abilities and bearing essentially the same message. They are well spaced in time, and the most recent may well be in living memory: Sri Satya Sai Baba.

A further repeated injunction is to keep the deity, or a universal consciousness, constantly in mind. In pondering this, the Walker returns to the scientific conclusions that the universe seems carefully created so that life could develop, Mind can influence matter and life itself is more likely than not to be deliberately created. Humankind appears to be the only earthly species conscious of its own consciousness and, therefore, potentially conscious of another, possibly higher, consciousness. Given these, anything good for humankind is good for the purposes of the Primal Mind if these include humankind's consciousness of that Primal Mind, and this seems to be the consistent gist of the Messengers.

How may ongoing mindfulness of the Primal Mind be good for that entity? Perhaps to stay connected with and guide its creation, in a manner reinforced by meditation. Many people are naturally helpful or prone to random acts of kindness, and this could be directed usefully. A peaceful, even loving, environment (coherent thought-patterns?) is crucial for the maintenance of a meditative state, and so an ethical society is more conducive to that connection. The same calm state is crucial for the manifestation of paranormal abilities. Theodicy ('tough love') holds that humankind must, if necessary, learn its lessons the hard way as do species by Darwinian selection, and if the precious entity here is the mind or soul rather than the human person, then the birth–death recycling makes sense, as do world wars, great plagues and natural disasters. They form part of the learning experience. The slow maturation of earthly human minds, finally not returning to Earth, allows the Primal Mind to grow and include personal experience of the material world, including the experience of time itself. In this sense, perhaps there is indeed an absolute standard of good and evil: if nothing exists except the Primal Mind and its creation, there is room for no other.

Conclusions from Science

The Walker summarises these three lines of inquiry, all seemingly counter to our common-sense experiences, respectively:

1. Mind (in the shape of observation) can affect energy (e.g., the wave property of light) to collapse it into particles, while energy (in the shape of matter) can affect other energy (entangled matter) non-locally (i.e., outside space-time).
2. The universe is singular and is composed *as if designed* to develop life with an unprecedentedly high certainty of departure from chance. Any other experimental situation would demand the conclusion that it *was* indeed so designed.
3. Wide-ranging paranormal phenomena are now shown to be real, far beyond any statistical or methodological doubt. This includes mind–energy (as matter) interactions (i.e., psychokinesis); mind–mind information transfer outside space-time (i.e., telepathy); mind–matter information transfer (i.e., perception at a distance, perception through time); and others.

Together, these show clearly that the mind, intention, thought, information, matter and energy do indeed all interact *outside space-time*, and humankind is intimately part of this. Lacking prejudice, the Walker concludes that, without doubt, the Mind came first and created matter in a way that allows the opportunity for life to develop. Knox's [5] equally familiar riposte to his own limerick quoted above is here almost startlingly apt:

> Dear Sir: your astonishment's odd.
> I am always about in the Quad.
> And that's why the tree
> Will continue to be,
> Since observed by, Yours faithfully, God.

Apt, that is, for fullerene molecules or smaller (which are small enough to be subject to Heisenberg's uncertainty principle), if not for Knox's tree or Einstein's moon (which are not).

Conclusions from Religion

The Walker sees that problems in religion are no fault of the Primal Mind, only humankind's inadequate understanding of the mystics' messages, an irresistible urge to over-elaborate and an innate tribal intolerance causing fragmentation. The Walker finds no rational basis for atheism or even strong scepticism (as opposed to the open mind of agnosticism), particularly as, logically, one cannot prove a negative proposition. Shorn of elaborations, the Messengers asked humankind to believe their word, their message. This was quite simple, unanimous and clear:

You are not a human being in search of a spiritual experience. You are a spiritual being immersed in a human experience. (Fr. Pierre Theilhard de Chardin, using language found identically in Hinduism.)

After this, you return to spirit. Hindus and Buddhists repeat this until 'graduation' to permanent residence; Judaeo-Christians and Muslims have no second chance at everlasting life. They repeatedly iterated rules of how humankind should live, which are simply exemplified in Sikhism, a fifteenth-century, monotheistic fusion of Hinduism and Islam:

- do good actions, do not perform rituals
- always keep God in heart and mind
- live honestly and work hard
- treat everyone equally
- be generous to the less fortunate
- serve others.

These rules are necessary for a happy, peaceful and mature society whose calmness is conducive to meditation and creative pursuits. Such benefits seem self-evident. The Walker sees this as crucial for further growth in relation of the Mind to humankind. The Messengers were no doubt compelling to their contemporaries, backed by apparent authority of the siddhis and their personalities, but this can fade over centuries with suspicion of the role of superstition. Elaboration, misinterpretation and editorial interference have blurred some messages, the whole set in stone as Holy Scripture that then must be accepted in toto.

Conclusions from Philosophy

The Walker sees philosophy has no conflict with science since its reasoning is based on sound observation, although they do not overlap in all areas. However, philosophy can conflict with religion on the grounds of reasoning since religions' premises are based on allegations with the character of assumptions.

SYNTHESIS

Science and philosophy are so inextricably entwined that it seems any outcome must be convergent. Are science and religion ultimately compatible? The answer would seem to be no in the absence of supporting evidence. However, within the last two decades the three scientific selections of the Walker have fully supplied that evidence, supporting the basic premises of the Messengers while noting that various aspects can have various names: Primal Mind, One Mind, intelligence, God, spirit, soul and others. The open-minded Walker is left in no doubt that this is the way the universe works. Finally, a striking concordance between science and religion is found in the most profound aspects of QM and meditative absorption, respectively: the essential unity of everything, all is part of One and vice versa.

The Walker concludes that the three meridians of science, religion and philosophy have indeed come together as the twenty-first century dawns. The meeting point is the Primal Mind. Instead of ignoring the Mind-first paradigm, cosmologists could do well to consider what effect this would have on their equations. It is also to be hoped that humankind recognises this more widely, and quickly.

Finally, the gist of Lester Smith's 1975 well-known introductory quotation:

> The universe begins to look more like a great thought than a great machine ... we are beginning to suspect ... [Mind] as the creator and governor of the realm of matter.
> (Sir James Jeans FRS, *The Mysterious Universe, 1930*)

An atheist might rephrase this as 'in the beginning was the meme'.

REFERENCES

1. Lester Smith, E., Ed., (1975). *Intelligence came first.* Quest Books, The Theosophical Publishing House, Wheaton, IL, USA.
2. Schrödinger, E. (1944). *What is Life?* and *Mind and Matter,* Cambridge University Press.
3. Heisenberg, W. (1958). *Physics and Philosophy,* Allen and Unwin.
4. Chiribella, G., D'Ariano, G. & Perinotti, P. (2011). *Informational Derivation of Quantum Theory.* Physical Review A, 84: 1-39.
5. Langford Reed (1924). *The Complete Limerick Book.*
6. Dawkins, R. (2006). *The God Delusion.* Transworld Publishers, London.

7. Flew, A. (2007). *There Is a God: How the World's Most Notorious Atheist Changed His Mind.* With R.A. Varghese. Harper Collins e-books.
8. *Yoga sutras of Patanjali.* Presented by Swami Jnaneshvara Bharati, www.SwamiJ.com
9. Levy P. (2018). *The Quantum Revelation: A Radical Synthesis of Science and Spirituality.* New York SelectBooks Inc.
10. Danby, L.C. (1974). *The certainty of eternity as revealed by the mediumship of a Melbourne carpenter.* Hill of Content Publishing, Melbourne.
11. Edwards. H. (1962). *The Mediumship of Jack Webber.* The Anchor Press Ltd, Tiptree, Essex, UK.
12. Murphet, H. (1973). *Sai Baba. Man of miracles.* Samuel Weiser Inc., New York, NY.
13. Sandweiss, S.H. (1975). *The holy man and the psychiatrist.* Birth Day Publishing, San Diego CA.
14. Haraldsson, E. (2013). *Modern Miracle: Sathya Sai Baba - the Story of a Modern Day Prophet.* White Crow Books, Guildford UK.

Chapter 3
The Puzzle – Why Is Everything So 'Just Right'?

"I believe in miracles: Something sacred burning in every bush and tree…" Joan Baez and Steve Clark

"In my Father's house there are many rooms." John 14 v.2

A Real Fifth Dimension?

SUMMARY

The science behind the design question is considered in greater detail, firstly for the material universe and secondly for the machinery of life. Once again, the enormity of the statistical odds against chance being responsible for origins becomes clear. The possibility of a multiverse is prohibited because the likelihood of occurrence by chance of an infinite number of events of probabilities less than one is zero. There is no rational alternative to space as the immediate source of life on Earth, via cometary biology and panspermia. The ultimate source is the ultimate mystery. There is no rational alternative to a conscious intent by some Primal Mind to obtain the machinery of the material universe and the miracle of material life. There is something sacred burning in every bush and tree.

In addition, the observed phenomena of quantum entanglement, quantum tunnelling, the quantum observer effect on wave–particle duality and the huge field of psychic and mediumistic effects show beyond doubt that the universe has dimensions in addition to the four of Einstein's space-time. These have to do with thought, consciousness and universal awareness. Science does not have a satisfactory theory to accommodate these.

Ever since humans realised that they were distinct conscious beings, it seems they wondered about their place in nature. Each preliterate culture developed its own rationalisation of how what it saw around came to be, handed on as oral history, often with a sacred spiritual basis involving discarnate ancestry and becoming an integral part of daily life.

In the East, the relation of humankind to Mind and consciousness dominated, with major advances in their understanding. In the Middle East and Europe, the focus became a prescribed view of the universe based on one tribal, spiritual and folk-memory history that was eventually backed by powerful, established Judaeo–Christian–Islamic churches that prohibited other forms of thought. This view was only seriously challenged after two millennia when some outstandingly able men in Europe made careful measurements with better instruments and open minds. Gradually, the spiritual connection faded, especially in the rigorously sceptical scientific environment where all needs to be proved by experiment. By the end of the nineteenth century, all seemed mapped out to Western science as a rational material clockwork universe. This attitude is still surprisingly widespread, and concepts of mind and spirit in science seem unnecessary, even dangerously atavistic and heretical. Mind and spirit are okay in their place.

In the first half of the twentieth century, the Western scientific worldview was shaken by the solid findings of relativity and QM in physics and genetic theory in biology, followed in the second half by the complete solving of the genetic code and much of the basic chemical machinery of living processes. Over time, these have all raised major questions on the nature of the way everything is. It is becoming increasingly difficult to maintain a purely materialistic worldview [1,2]. While we remain forever constrained by the limits of human imagination, we still strive to extract something that *we* can understand from the shadows in Plato's cave. This forces us to conceive beyond the material, and humankind's contemplative journey returns to its roots, except that we have more know-how and freedom to follow the evidence. Our problem now is to choose between the possible and the new rational.

THE DESIGN QUESTION – THE MATERIAL UNIVERSE

While we may take our fertile planet for granted, it turns out that the cosmic conditions for its very existence are extremely unusual [3]. At least six cosmic parameters have to be so finely tuned that the overall tolerances cannot vary by more than 1 in 10^{200}. In addition, over 80 further critical parameters have more recently been proposed for the universe at large, and more than 150 other features for the nearer region of our galaxy and planetary system, all of which must be exact within narrow margins for life to be feasible [4].

There are three possible causes of such an outcome: necessity or natural law; chance or random actions; intention or action of a creative Mind. Of these, no relevant natural law has been found (although one may possibly emerge), chance is reduced to impossibly low levels and only intention remains. At present, it seems some Mind went to great lengths to achieve the possibility of carbon and water–based life somewhere in the known universe.

An attempt to reintroduce chance came with the multiverse concept, where one of an infinite number of different universes can provide by accident the unique universe we need. But this was a non-falsifiable, non-evidenced conjecture and does not survive a closer look [5]. Our universe being extremely improbable, any universe slightly outside its limited parameters will be similarly unlikely, and an infinite collection of improbabilities will surely be infinitely improbable, whatever that means. This conclusion is better expressed in probability theory: the chance of occurrence of two or more random events is the product of their individual probabilities. The product of an infinite array of numbers less than unity is zero, and so an infinite multiverse is prohibited. There are also cogent philosophical and mathematical reasons to expect a singular universe and the reality of time [6].

We are left only with the appearance of intention, implying a creative Mind.

THE DESIGN QUESTION – THE MACHINERY OF LIFE

Similar issues of necessity, chance or intention relate to the origin and complexity of living things on Earth. No natural law is presently known that compels life; indeed, the second law of thermodynamics seems to forbid such a spontaneous increase in information content. Yet water *can* flow uphill; witness the green belt above the waterfall's pool wetted only by misty droplets raised by its kinetic energy. We also know that biology uses chemical energy to reverse the second law, but this needs complex chemical machinery that cannot be built without pre-existing chemical energy, raising the classical chicken-and-egg problem that bedevils origins in all of biology. Factors cumulatively dismissing chance theory are recently exhaustively and critically summarised by Meyer [7,8]. While chemical bonds can form by chance, especially under electrical discharge, volcanic heat and/or a catalytic surface, the chance of soon being unmade seems at least as great. The total number of chemical bonds formed in the known universe since its beginning cannot exceed the product of its total number of elementary particles (10^{80}), its age ($< 10^{19}$ seconds, according to the SC) and the greatest number of translocations a particle can achieve per second (10^{43}; i.e., the number of Planck lengths, or the smallest quantum distance possible, contained in the distance covered by light per second). This equals $< 10^{143}$, or very conservatively $< 10^{150}$ (Dembski), dubbed the 'probabilistic resource of the Universe'.

Such an unimaginably large number (1 followed by 150 zeros) is nevertheless easily exceeded if one calculates the number of random bond formations needed to produce any sort of cellular machinery by chance. To create only one accurate L copy of all 20 amino acids with their inevitable D isomers would require a total of 10^{132} random bonds. As many more than one copy each is needed, already we are well over the limit of probabilistic resource, assuming that all universe-wide bonds attempted are directed to earthly amino acid formation. Selecting the right candidates from this huge pool of 'junk' molecules to form even one tiny peptide hormone by chance is clearly impossible. Further, this does not account for the additional improbability of creating by chance even a simple protein with the necessary structural stability to possess any function, let alone one with a particular function, or the 250–400 specific functions needed for even the simplest microorganism (mycoplasma). The mathematical calculations to predict the amino acid sequence needed to make just one of the many proteins in a polymerase complex is staggering. Then we start to consider the astoundingly clever, computer-like features of the genetic code; information-tape structure of DNA and RNA; replication, transcription and translation of this information; epigenetic information transfer; membrane and organelle structure; and more. Darwinian evolution and selection work well for the origin of species, as originally proposed, but not for the origin of life itself, as Darwin was himself aware.

Much has been made of the potential for neo-Darwinism to produce new genetic information, but it cannot do so to that extent. Mutation and selection only work on pre-existing genetic information, and there has not been enough evolutionary time to copy and modify that much software. In addition, the fossil record shows that almost all animal phyla appeared relatively suddenly in the Cambrian and late pre-Cambrian eras, embodying copious new genetic information. Contrary to expectation from neo-Darwinian theory, diversification within animal phyla occurred 'top-down': phyla did not evolve from multiple forms with small differences in characters but, rather, emerged relatively suddenly as fully fledged phyla differing in very many properties, then split into classes, then orders, then families, etc.

This conundrum is neatly solved by the Hoyle–Wickramasinghe solution of cometary panspermia [9], which is discussed in the next section of this chapter. The paper of Steele et al. (2018) [10] focuses on the Cambrian emergence of retroviruses, the remarkable evolution of the intelligent complexity of cephalopods and the microfossil evidence contained within meteorites.

But these data raise another important question. Scholarly texts on the origin of multicellularity, if deemed worth mentioning, may simply assert that it evolved from unicellularity. Research projects tacitly assume so with no justification for why. Such views are encouraged by the well-supported development in eukaryotic cells of endosymbiosis by the engulfment of once-independent prokaryotic microbes to form mitochondria and chloroplasts [11]. Examples are quoted of cooperative associations of microbes under certain adverse conditions (e.g., the amoebal slime mould *Dictyostelium*, the alga *Volvox* and the bacterium *Pseudomonas*), but these appear more as special survival strategies of intrinsically unicellular organisms. Nevertheless, the very large differences between prokaryotic and eukaryotic organisation and content of genetic material do not suggest such a simple origin for eukaryotic cells, and this question appears unanswered. Could it be that such evolution did not occur at all, and we are looking at another quantum leap in design where intention is the only valid explanation? This issue deserves the same careful analysis as given to the evolution of life and phyla by Meyer.

No explanations appear either for why it took so long to get to multicellularity in the two billion years since enough oxygen was produced to precipitate all iron out of seawater. Possibly, the delay was simply to build up enough microbial resources of amino acids to sustain a higher food chain. In fact, the developmental series produced, in a logical order, a food chain to sustain advanced life forms –first, unicellular microbes able to synthesise metabolic needs from sunlight and simple molecules, then filter-feeders of microbes (e.g., sponges, tunicate worms, some molluscs), then predators of these more advanced forms (e.g., chordates and arthropods).

Thus, the chance creation of life is no longer a possibility worth considering. Even confirmed sceptics now often accept the *appearance* of design while failing to suppose, or even denying, any cause. Again, there is no rational alternative to the idea that some Mind went to great lengths to actualise carbon and water–based life forms on our home planet. Both the foregoing sections inevitably lead to the conclusion that this creative Mind should exist, at least in part, outside its creation, that is, *outside space-time*.

THE HOYLE–WICKRAMASINGHE VERSION OF COSMIC COMETARY BIOLOGY

Recent developments on Earth (as of March 2020 AD) give immediacy to the phenomenon of panspermia. As mentioned earlier in this chapter, the development of life on Earth by chance is so improbable as not even worth mentioning. The only real question is: if so, where did life come from, and how did it get here? There is only one resource, whether it seems rational or not: space. In fact, it is very persuasive and, lacking an alternative, conclusive [9].

The concept of panspermia was familiar to classical Greeks. In essence, it proposes that interstellar space contains a multitude of organisms, appropriately protected, that act as seeds to start life on whatever planet they may land. Their source comprises older planets that, for various reasons, constantly shed these seeds into space. Their ultimate origins are as mysterious as the One Mind itself (see Chapter 1).

Modern support, inspired by the Hoyle–Wickramasinghe concept and based on astronomical observations during 1986–2018 [9], includes the following. There are huge amounts of microbial material in space, as evidenced by the close superposition (a) of the infrared spectra of radiation from the galactic centre and desiccated bacteria and (b) of the total extinction (absorption + scattering) of astronomical data points for interstellar dust and light passing through an artificial mixture of viral and bacterial dust. The presence of large amounts of microbial material on the surface of the International Space

Station at altitudes (411 km) higher than the ceiling for micron-sized atmospheric dust [12] was surprising, although it cannot be proved that this is inbound.

Equally significant are modern probes of cometary bodies [9]. Cometary nuclei can be coal-like and not icy. The dust coma of Halley's comet, observed on 31 March 1986 with the Anglo-Australian Telescope, emitted radiation over the range 2.0–4.0 micrometres that was almost completely superimposable with dried *Escherichia coli*, whether X-irradiated or not. The Giotto space probe to Halley's comet showed a very dark carbon-rich surface of a peanut-shaped body 15 km long and 7–10 km wide, with outgassing jets shedding three tonnes per second. Similarly, the Rosetta mission's Philae lander on comet 67P/C-G did not show a hard-frozen, non-biological nucleus. The reflectivity spectra of the surface were similar to biological material. The infrared spectrum from Comet Hale-Bopp (1997, 60 km in diameter) matched microbial mixtures with some clay-like dust and a prodigious output of organic dust and carbon monoxide radiating at 6.5 angstrom units that indicated the high-pressure release of material from a liquified subsurface where microbes could flourish. A very similar spectrum was found in the post-impact ejecta from the Deep Impact mission (2005) to comet 9P/Tempel. These are all inconsistent with simple chemistry but consistent with cometary biology. Microbes can be famously space hardy, especially if protected by carbonaceous matter or ice.

In early 2020, the whole of humanity was locked down in the greatest pandemic since the Spanish flu of 1918–1922: the COVID-19 pandemic. More informatively, it can be termed SARS-CoV-2, linked to the closely related SARS-CoV-1 of 2002–2003. A few weeks before both outbreaks, bright cometary meteoroids were seen in the Irkutsk region of Siberia (late September 2002) and in Jilin, China (October 2019) [13. These locations are < 2500 km apart.

The earliest cases of SARS-CoV-2 in a particular area tell a revealing story [13]. No 'case zero' has been found despite intense efforts, and animal sources or 'wet markets' can be discounted. It seems that many people were simultaneously infected in Hubei province, especially Wuhan city, in early November 2019. Subsequent infections show a clear westerly time sequence from discrete epicentres in South Korea, Iran, the Lombardy region in Italy, and New York, all close to latitude 30–50 degrees N. These infections all happened at least 27 days after the lockdown in Wuhan (23 January 2020).

Because the worldwide caseload was small, tracing SARS-CoV-1 was less reliable [14]. It was first reported in Guangdong province, South China, on 16 November 2002. By 15 February 2003, it had spread, person-to-person by travellers, to nearby Hong Kong. Notably, all nearby regions reported their first cases close together: 23 February in Vietnam and 25 February in Taiwan, the Philippines and Singapore. The proximity of the travel hub Hong Kong probably explains its early appearance in the United States (9 January), then Canada (23 February). Fortunately, SARS-CoV-1 was a failure as a pandemic agent despite high infectivity and mortality, probably because of high morbidity that reduced patient mobility. Too sick to party.

Finally, the Wickramasinghe-associated research group has adduced massive support [15] for a concept with which the lead author, Ted Steele, has been involved for 50 years, namely neo-Lamarckian inheritance in plants, animals and microbes, based on copious published work. This is dependent on six lines of evidence: (1) environmental stimulation as the directional mutation driver, (2) epigenetic targeting, (3) rapid genetic adaptation, (4) penetration of the Weismann barrier, (5) horizontal gene transfer, and (6) the central role of reverse transcription (involving retroviruses). Item (5) is illustrated by the well-known and ready transfer of antibiotic resistance by genetic recombination among pathogenic bacteria that greatly affects the clinical armoury, incidentally illustrating item (4), the leakiness of the Weismann Barrier.

Clearly, the ability to select and integrate large segments of useful DNA with associated epigenetic flexibility rather than relying on blind mutation and selection could enormously speed-up adaptation to an alien environment if that organism should fall on a strange planet.

These mechanisms for panspermia demand the planet-wide distribution of trillions of particles, as large as plant seeds and fertilised ova and as small as individual virions. Their feasibility on Earth is plausibly explained by westerly stratospheric winds and a winter downdraft, demonstrated by radioactive tracers incorporated in the last atmospheric nuclear test on 11 August 1958. The origin of the fiery boloids of 2002 and 2019 is probably the Orionid meteor shower shed by Halley's comet, which Earth crosses every year in late October – early November. It coincides with the regular recurrence of northern respiratory illnesses, such as seasonal influenza and respiratory syncytial virus.

Planet Earth's dependence on its ambient space is emphasised by the Cretaceous-Tertiary extinction, generally thought to be caused by the impact of a 10–15 km comet or asteroid on the Chicxulub peak ring on the Yucatan Peninsula, Gulf of Mexico, 66 million years ago. It caused a lingering winter that halted photosynthesis in plants and plankton. In the geological record, there is a worldwide thin layer of sediment (the K-Pg boundary) containing high levels of iridium, more common in asteroids than the Earth's crust. This opened the opportunity for mammals to flourish and diversify. One is left to wonder if the non-avian dinosaurs proved unable to evolve mentally, and the universe took action accordingly.

While much of this evidence may seem circumstantial, the odds against cumulative chance occurrences are, appropriately enough, astronomical.

QUANTUM ENTANGLEMENT

A pair of elementary particles, such as electrons, that have been intimately connected (e.g., simultaneously expelled from the same atom) remain so even if separated by kilometres, such that if one of the pair is altered, the other is also identically changed. The effect was predicted from quantum theory [16] and subsequently verified by experiment [17,18]. This connection occurs simultaneously and is considered *outside space-time*.

QUANTUM TUNNELLING

Isaac Newton saw a strange optical effect while exploring the total internal reflection of light in prisms. If a second smooth glass surface was in intimate contact with the prism's reflecting surface, then internal reflection did not occur, but if that second surface was separated by a tiny distance (~1 nanometre) internal reflection returned, as expected. But not completely: a little light 'jumped' the gap, the amount dropping sharply as the gap increased. This effect, now termed 'frustrated total internal reflection', is related to wavelength; an 'evanescent wave' is created on the first surface that induces a corresponding real wave in the adjacent surface that can be measured. However, the inducing effect occurs in almost zero time, that is, it crosses at many times the speed of light [19]. This was recently shown more clearly by Nimtz and Stahlhofen [20], using tea-chest sized acrylic prisms and microwaves to obtain a jumpable gap of ~10 cm. In a related system, Nimtz's group showed that an actual information signal (a Mozart symphony) was transmitted many times faster than light. This seems to run counter to relativity theory and so is high heresy, but, in fact, causality was shown to be non-violated. 'Trevelyan' [19] extended the gap to 4 metres by using pulsed radio waves and the concept that the gap represents a timeless zone (eternity box) outside space-time. Possibly, electromagnetic radiation cannot 'see' anything outside space-time and so cannot exist there, translating to virtual photons (?) to get across. Either view has interesting possible connotations. The point for us is that information can be sent *outside space-time*.

NON-LOCAL CONSCIOUSNESS – THE QUANTUM OBSERVER EFFECT ON WAVE–PARTICLE DUALITY

Although not hard for many people, one of the most intuitively difficult ideas for scientists to swallow has been that of 'spooky' (Einstein) mental action at a distance. ('There is no theoretical basis, and surely neural action must be confined to the brain?') However, we have shown that non-local effects are well established for other systems. Possibly the best-documented (and most hotly debated) mainstream scientific topic relating to this is the QM observer effect. Here, the characteristic wave-like behaviour of small particles (electrons, photons, atoms and small molecules, such as fullerene) is collapsed to particle behaviour apparently by the simple act of extracting information (observation).

Radin and colleagues [21] (see Chapter 1) reported rigorously controlled replications of the QM observer effect using double-slit and Michelson interferometer apparatus [22]. They found results with double-digit significance using a random set of subjects but with highly experienced meditators showing odds against chance of $> 10^5$ to one in individual tests and $> 10^9$ to one overall. Wave behaviour can certainly be collapsed to particles by simply applying the mind to it, *outside space-time*. Unfortunately, sceptics will have a problem with replicating this, as it will depend on finding (and persuading) this rare type of subject.

These data now seem to settle this debate affirmatively once and for all (provided someone is courageous enough to replicate them). Von Neumann first offered the 'consciousness' interpretation of QM in 1932, modified by Wigner in 1960 and supported through the twentieth century by other prominent scientists. It remains an open question for mainstream science, with a small minority of experts still strongly supporting it [23]. The objections seem largely ideological: since it is 'impossible' there 'must' be some unidentified flaw in apparatus or interpretation. It has proved a difficult idea to debunk, and although alternative interpretations were feasible, none seemed entirely satisfactory [24]. Mainstream science originally objected to the QM observer effect, largely because it posits a non-material Mind existing at all times in the history of the universe, contrary to the worldview of many scientists. In light of the first two sections above, at least, this objection is no longer tenable. It will be interesting to see how long it takes for the mainstream to catch up with the awareness of post-materialist science. Meanwhile, the following section puts this old argument into a more general context.

PSYCHIC PHENOMENA (PSI)

The most compelling and the most scientifically controversial (for reasons given in the previous section) set of data relevant to our topic is probably the broad field of psi studies. Although a common experience of a surprisingly large number of people but hitherto taboo for serious science, the importance of mental attention on material objects and other minds in understanding the universe is becoming very evident.

The confusion caused by 'stage magic' and deliberate fraud has been settled by over a century of carefully chosen methodology and relentless criticism leading to repeated refinement [25,26]. The most useful have been small psi effects repeatable indefinitely in normal subjects and suitable for statistical evaluation. These have been exploited in thousands of replicate tests to show that information can be transmitted mentally over macroscopic distances in virtually zero time, and material devices, such as thrown dice and random number generators, can be influenced by attention alone. Radin's meticulous analysis [26] shows that in each case of telepathy, clairvoyance or micro-psychokinesis (effects of mind on mind or on matter, respectively) statistical analysis shows the odds in favour of chance to be vanishingly small, in one case less than one in a billion. Precognition and presentience are demonstrated. Psi effects can be much larger and statistically more impressive if experienced meditators are the subjects. Minds can seem to be 'entangled', especially if couples are emotionally bonded. It is further shown that individual minds can reinforce each other, and a mass field effect exists when very large numbers of people are focused on one theme. Importantly, psi effects are greatest when the system reaches higher coherence, or greater degree of order.

Thus, the question of the reality of psi is settled, scientifically speaking; mind can undoubtedly affect matter or other minds *outside space-time.*

We could, if we wish, rest our case here with this proof of principle firmly in place, but there is much more to account for. Larger, quasi-anecdotal mediumistic experiences or effects [27,28,29], observed many times by small groups within reliable recent testimony but dependent on a specially gifted person (medium), are difficult to assess rigorously but are too numerous and challenging to ignore. While dependent on the credibility, goodwill and serious-mindedness of the mostly lay people present (often observing sceptically), such studies fulfil the criteria of repeatability and objective observability. In these respects, they do not differ from more formal scientific tests, except they are more vulnerable to allegations of fraud. Like other psi phenomena, they require a quiet, emotionally neutral or coherent, even sympathetic, environment, which probably explains why so many 'formal' laboratory tests of psi have failed. Such data are not readily suited to statistical analysis but are supported in some cases by photographs (e.g., of ectoplasm or levitation), material objects (apports, psychic paintings) and written testimonies.

More common are personal experiences, highly persuasive for the person involved – difficult to assess yet impossible to ignore. Their value scientifically lies in their sheer abundance, context, cumulative conformity and perceived reliability of the narrator/witnesses. They have been termed meaningful coincidences (synchronicities) [30], NDEs [31] or out-of-body experiences. In addition, multiple instances providing evidence for reincarnation [32] are cumulatively impossible to ascribe to chance.

Finally, there is a very controversial group that is historically illuminating, centring on the entertainer Uri Geller in the mid-1970s. To use his undoubted psi talents [31] as he did was a disservice to science: some 'spoon-bending' may well have been real at times if cheating at others. However, after his appearance on British television, there was a rash of young 'benders' presenting Geller-like claims. Taylor's first book [34] described this phenomenon and may well have contained some gems, but any subsequent program was (probably illegally) sabotaged by a notorious sceptic and stage magician's planting of skilled conjurors among Taylor's subjects to reveal his inexperience of trickery. His disgrace was followed by a somewhat unconvincing recantation [35] of his belief in the reality of psi with undertones of pressures like Galileo's inquisition. Whether or not this was a service to science, the scandal (and the gleeful sceptics) was definitely not, especially to similar work published later by the respected experimental physicist John Hasted [36], which received unwarranted criticism. For example, the objection (treated as decisive) that the subject was not secretly camera-recorded during the 'wires in the bottle' experiments is silly and irrelevant unless a viable way around Hasted's careful precautions is offered. This whole affair illustrates the vicious nature of the debate. In fact, one cannot read Hasted's book without knowing that 'something very interesting was going on'; readers realise that one cannot sit down elbow-to-elbow with a subject as Hasted did and be deceived all the time. It is relevant here to search Dean Radin's book on psi phenomena [22] for 'But it did happen'.

Is this enough scientifically? Yes and no. Sceptics are quick to bury an entire body of work because some of it is not perfect, losing both baby and bath water. Is it legitimate to cherry-pick the data? Scientists are divided on this; clearly, if one aspect is uncertain, then it is wise to look closely at the rest. My view is yes, of course, if the cherry itself can be deemed sound. But then it is incumbent on the pickers to give the rest careful weight, preferably to check it out themselves. Being able to accept that psi is real encourages us to spend time and money on cherries, learn something valuable and follow it up.

While not exactly a waste of time, humankind has spent the better part of a century arguing about the very existence of psi. We now have a host of affirmative data, and it is time to find some kind of unifying theory.

DISCUSSION

We are left with an extraordinary proposition. Like the rest of us, Newton naturally recognised the three dimensions of space, and – since Einstein's insights – science has readily absorbed the concept of space-time, with time as a fourth dimension. Our confronting concept now is that there is certainly some further quality, aspect, feature or property that is 'outside' space-time (as outlined above, at least). What does 'outside space-time' mean? It seems to permeate the whole of space-time, including in two cases at least our persons where the affecting entity seems to be intention, or thought, or mind. Thoughts are like things.

Whatever kind of 'thing' can thought be? Some kind of informational pattern must be involved, and the only kinds of carriers for it in our ken are those we regard as 'inside space-time'. It seems we need a new concept for this too, something outside our ken. Here one wonders about the mysterious inductive radiation suggested to carry Mozart's thoughts by quantum tunnelling *outside space-time*.

What theoretical basis can there be for such phenomena? Our conjectured proposal here is that our visible universe is simply immersed, like a porous bubble of space-time, in a more vast, unknowable continuum that also permeates the bubble and behaves like a fifth dimension but contains thought. We could call it consciousness or universal awareness. Having accepted the invention of time as a fourth dimension, there seems no rational objection to the possibility of a fifth (or more). It is not necessarily a medium, as that would imply a carrier material, as air and water are carriers for sound. It is just a dimension in which thoughts or minds exist as information carriers. Maybe thoughts form the basis of matter in space-time, and matter is created, possibly also maintained, from/by energy.

In fact, extra dimensions are no novelty in cosmology. The two sacred icons of twentieth-century physics, special/general relativity and QM theories (each thoroughly sound in mathematics and experiment), could only be combined and reconciled by something like superstring theory [37], which demands no less than six dimensions more than the four of space-time. This theory proposes that the 12 basic particles of matter (four types each of electrons, neutrinos and quarks) fall naturally into a unified pattern if conceived as specific vibration modes (equivalent to pitch and tone of a musical instrument) of a single, fundamental one-dimensional particle (a 'string', no shorter than the Planck length, 10^{-33} cm). These modes confer energy and, thus, mass ($E = mc^2$), calculable by combined relativity and QM theory and confirmed by experiment. This idea also works well with the messenger particles by which the four major forces are supposed to be transmitted. However, superstring theory involves approximations, better resolved by M-theory and brane theory, which in turn require vibrations in one more (eleventh) dimension. Such theories give useful unifications of diverse data but are not currently regarded as the complete answer. They remain just theories.

We find it hard to conceive just one extra dimension, let alone the seven now expected of us. Perhaps we never can. They have been pictured in terms of multiple surface geometries *inside* space-time, although, intuitively, they should somehow be intermeshed or co-permeable with, or even outside/containing, the others. Such extra dimensions remain hypothetical and, accordingly, exist only as useful mathematical abstractions, like the square root of minus one. For now, they should be regarded as imaginary dimensions instead of the real ones of space-time (begging the philosophical problem of the nature of reality). Possibly that stupendous mathematical Mind in designing the material universe and life itself used the same convenient abstractions, or perhaps this is how everything really is – imaginary.

What are the essential properties of our proposed fifth dimension? It must at least have extent and capacity (for content) but not time as we know it. We do not currently have the concepts to imagine what these may be. Our strongest clues may be the almost ineffable descriptions of 'heaven' returned to us by the thousands of NDEs and mediumistic experiences reported, with their hints of yet higher 'planes' or 'spheres' (or perhaps dimensions). If string theory is really relevant, then, presumably, QM still applies in heaven.

Quite recently, Neppe and Close [38,39] offered a refreshingly novel approach that anticipates our thesis. They had discovered that an obscure but long-known constant in particle physics (the Cabibbo angle) could be mathematically derived using a nine-dimensional vortical spin model, but no other number would work except, perhaps, some harmonic of nine. Reasoning that this should be an important and profound aspect of a theory of everything and recognising (from their own psychiatric work, at least) the reality of psi, they constructed a hypothesis notionally allotting three dimensions each to space, time and consciousness. The core tenet is that all three are inseparably, *always*, tethered in all things across and between dimensions, albeit to variable degrees of tightness. This was developed mathematically and termed Triadic Dimensional Distinction Vortical Paradigm. It is argued (as here) that the easiest way to explain psi is by accepting the existence of higher dimensions. The value and/or proof of a hypothesis lie in its predictive power; several such 'proofs' are claimed and published, but it is too soon to expect independent validation or evaluation of the hypothesis generally. Neppe and Close say they are seeking an extension of special relativity to include a nine-dimensional finite reality with triadic quarks and relevance to life elements.

The sense of closeness to a universal theory of everything is currently exciting theoretical physicists, but this cannot hope to succeed unless it accommodates *all* the data. Many findings outlined above clearly comprise relevant hard data, and it continues to be absurd, even irresponsible, to see them still ignored. The Neppe–Close paradigm seems to take us a giant step further but can expect major resistance at best and major indifference at worst.

What kind of test could falsify a higher dimension? Certainly not Neppe–Close or relativity or QM, which predict, even demand it – in spades. Of course, one or more of these dimensions might be proven to have the properties of universal awareness in time. Now that would be really exciting.

CONCLUSIONS

The scientific fields of enquiry encompassed by (1) the designs of the universe, (2) the machinery of life, (3) quantum entanglement, (4) quantum tunnelling, (5) the observer effect on quantum uncertainty, and (6) psychic studies all indicate some entity or quality that is *outside space-time*. While not necessarily all the same, science needs some theoretical concept to deal with them. Four at least have an integral connection with the operation of the mind. We simply propose the existence of a higher dimension(s), equivalent to consciousness or universal awareness, to accommodate thought in addition to the four of space-time. In part, this is anticipated by the reconciliation of relativity and quantum theories by string, M-theory or brane theories and by the Neppe–Close hypothesis, which demand something like it.

REFERENCES

1. Tart CT. *The End of Materialism.* Oakland, CA, Petaluma, CA: New Harbinger Publishers, Institute of Noetic Sciences; 2009.
2. Dossey L. *One Mind. How our Individual Mind is part of a Greater Consciousness and Why it Matters.* Carlsbad, CA: Hay House Inc; 201
3. Rees MJ. *Just Six Numbers: the Deep Forces that shape the Universe.* London: Weidenfeld and Nicholson; 1999.
4. Williams SJ. *What your Atheist Professor Doesn't Know (But Should).* RFH; 2009.
5. Cooper, PD. The Multiverse Paradox: Infinite Parallel Universes Are Impossible Cosmology 19: 62-68; 2015. http://cosmology.com/PeterCooperMultiverse.pdf
6. Unger MB, Smolin L. *The Singular Universe and the Reality of Time. A proposal in Natural Philosophy.* Cambridge: Cambridge University Press; 2015.
7. Meyer SC. *Signature in the cell: DNA and the evidence for Intelligent Design.* Sydney: Harper Collins; 2009.
8. Meyer SC. *Darwin's doubt: the explosive origin of animal life and the case for Intelligent Design* and *Epilogue.* Sydney: HarperCollins. 2013 and 2014.
9. Wickramasinghe NC, Wickramasinghe DT, Tout CA, Lattanzio JC, Steele EJ. (2019). Cosmic biology in perspective. *Astrophysics and Space Science,* 364(11),[205]. https://doi.org/10.1007/s10509-019-3698-6
10. Steele EJ and 31 others. (2018). Cause of Cambrian Explosion - Terrestrial or Cosmic? *Prog Biophys Mol Biol* 136: 3-23. https://doi.org/10.1016/j.pbiomolbio.2018.03.004
11. *It Takes Teamwork: How Endosymbiosis Changed Life on Earth.* www.evolution.berkeley.edu/evolibrary/article/endosymbiosis

12. Wickramasinghe, NC. Rycroft MJ. Wickramasinghe DT, Steele EJ, Wallis DH, Temple R, Tokoro G, Syroeshkin AV, Grebennikova TV, Tsygankov OS. (2018.) Confirmation of Microbial Ingress from Space. *Adv. Astrophysics* 3(4):266- 270.
13. Wickramasinghe NC, Steele EJ, Gorczynski RM, Temple R, Tokoro G, Kondakov A, Wallis DH, Klyce B, Wickramasinghe DE. (2020) Predicting the Future Trajectory of COVID-19. *Virol Curr Res* 4, 1-6. https://doi:10.37421/virolcurrres.2020.4.111
14. WHO Summary Table of SARS Cases by Country, 1 November 2002– 7 August 2003. www.who.int/csr/sars/country/country2003_08_15.pdf
15. Steele, E.J, Gorczynski RM, Lindley RA, Liu Y, Wickramasinghe NC (2019). Lamarck and Panspermia - On the Efficient Spread of Living Systems Throughout the Cosmos. *Prog Biophysics Mol Bio*, 149 10-32. https://doi.org/10.1016/j.pbiomolbio.2019.08.010
16. Bell JS. *On the Einstein Podolsky Rosen Paradox.* Physics. 1 (3): 195-200; 1964.
17. Freedman SJ, Clauser JF. *Experimental Test of Local Hidden-Variable Theories.* Phys Rev Lett, 28:938-941; 1972.
18. Aspect A, Grangier P, Roger G. *Experimental Realization of Einstein-Podolsky-Rosen-Bohm Gedankenexperiment.* Physical Review Letters, 49(2): 91-94; 1982.
19. Manley SM. *Eternity, God, Soul, New Physics.* Amazon Inc; 2013.
20. Nimtz, G. & Stahlhofen, A.A. (2008). Universal Tunnelling Time for all Fields. Ann. Phys. (Berlin) 17:374.
21. Radin D, Michel M, Galdamez K, Wendland P, Richenbach R, Delomi A. Consciousness and the Double–Slit Interference Pattern. Phys Essays 25(2): 157- 171; 2012.
22. Radin D. *Supernormal. Science, Yoga, and the Evidence for Extraordinary Psychic Abilities.* New York: Crown Publishing Group; 2013.
23. Schlosshauer M, Kofler J, Zeilinger A. A Snapshot of Foundational Attitudes Toward Quantum Mechanics. Stud Hist Phil Mod Phys. 44: 222-230; 2013.
24. Schreiber Z. The Nine Lives of Schrödinger's Cat. Univ London, Imperial College, Dept Physics Master's dissertation. arXiv:quant-ph/9501014v5 27 Jan 1995.
25. Radin D. *Entangled Minds. Extrasensory Experiences in a Quantum Reality.* New York: Paraview Pocket Books; 2006.
26. Radin D. *The Noetic Universe. The Scientific Evidence for Psychic Phenomena.* London: Transworld Publishers; 2009.

27. Smith-Moncrieffe D. *Medium7 Evidence of the Afterlife and Predictions.* Bloomington IN: iUniverse, Inc; 2013.
28. Danby LC. *The certainty of eternity as revealed by the mediumship of a Melbourne carpenter.* Melbourne: Hill of Content Publishing; 1974.
29. Edwards H. *The Mediumship of Jack Webber.* Tiptree, Essex: The Harry Edwards Spiritual Healing Sanctuary Trust; 1962.
30. Inglis B. *Coincidence. A Matter of Chance – or Synchronicity?* Guildford UK: White Crow Books Ltd; 2012.
31. Alexander E. *Proof of Heaven. A neurosurgeon's journey into the afterlife.* Sydney: Pan Macmillan Australia; 2012.
32. Stevenson I. *Twenty cases suggestive of reincarnation.* Charlottesville, VA: University of Virginia Press; 1974.
33. Panati C. ed. *The Geller Papers.* Boston MA: Houghton Miffin Co; 1976.
34. Taylor J. *Superminds. An investigation into the Paranormal.* London: Macmillan London Ltd; 1975.
35. Taylor J. *Science and the Supernatural. An Investigation of Paranormal Phenomena.* London: Granada Publishing Ltd; 1981.
36. Hasted JB. *The Metal Benders.* London: Routledge & Kegan Paul; 1981.
37. Greene B. *The Fabric of the Cosmos. Space, Time and the Texture of Reality.* London: Penguin Books Ltd; 2004.
38. Neppe VM, Close ER. *Reality Begins With Consciousness: A Paradigm Shift That Works.* ed. 5. Seattle: Brainvoyage.com; 2014.
39. Neppe VM, Close ER. The Concept of Relative Non-Locality: Theoretical Implications in Consciousness Research. Explore (NY). 2015; 11 (2): 102-10.

Chapter 4
The Answer: Purpose (naturally)

*...we cannot expect ever to find firm scientific proof of Purpose...
perhaps 'hope' is the difference between Sheep and Goats...
Many people today live without ultimate hope and don't know it.*

Purpose: A Slow Dawning for Us All?

I often think it comical (fah-la-la-lah ...)
How Nature always doth contrive (fah-la-la-lah)
That every boy and every gal that's born into this world alive
Is either a little Liberal or else a little Conservative
(fah-la-la-lah).
Sgt Willis, Iolanthe, W. S. Gilbert and A. Sullivan.

SUMMARY

Is your glass half full or half-empty? Is the universe randomly pointless? Many present-day scientists and philosophers think so; at least, they cannot see any purpose. They may be described as nihilists – there is nothing there.

Nihilists strive mightily to counter any philosophical or scientific evidence that a non-material dimension exists. 'Since there is nothing there, any evidence must be non-rational'. Why they battle so hard suggests a deep fear. The battle is illustrated in three categories: evidence for the paranormal; deliberate obfuscation of the isotope dating of the Turin Shroud; and evidence for reincarnation.

The material universe is so cleverly constructed that it is difficult to understand the lack of curiosity inherent in the absence of the why question. Perhaps it relates to our immaturity as a species. We need to moderate our behaviour spontaneously and hope that there is love and purpose, as the Messengers have told us. Many people live without ultimate hope and do not know it, caused in part by the fear-driven actions of the nihilists.

It may involve a leap of trust, like learning to walk and swim.

You will have noticed how some people usually expect good outcomes while others take the view that the 'glass is half-empty' – quite draining companions. In science seminars,

The Answer: Purpose (naturally)

some are interested in new ideas and are constructively critical, while others remain unimpressed. Some scientific colleagues and students assume a priori that nature is randomly pointless and others that it is purposeful. A professorial science friend and colleague, then unknowingly near the end of his life, once remarked to me, 'what's the point of it all?'

My worldview was fixed early with the astounding picture of the periodic table, the exquisite order making chemistry so much easier to grasp. Order to me spelled purpose, but it has taken decades more to figure out why it is actually more general. I once watched a squadron of lightning-fast swallows hunting swarms of tiny flying things over the lakeside. Their bodies were so clearly fit for purpose, as were their feast victims so fortuitously prolific. Such Darwinian adaptation exists all around.

So purpose does exist, but purpose demands some job not yet complete. Swallows do their bit for the food chain while humans are parasitic and could destroy it. Is there a deeper point to it all, for humans? Does it matter anyway?

As human populations reach critical mass and we see their problems made worse worldwide by climate change; personal and corporate greed; gross inequality; and a litany of other divisive issues, it is impossible to deny that this century will be critical for all life forms on Earth. If humanity could see even a hope of a higher purpose and be incentivised to follow it, then yes, it matters. No small task.

There is a large body of opinion in science that could be familiarly paraphrased as the Dawkins–Hawking Axis of Nihil. This opinion offers, literally, nothing, especially for purpose. Are there cogent scientific reasons to dispute nihilism?

Statutory warning: the following may be offensive to some readers and harmful to the careers of younger persons by affecting their granting bodies.

Early in the twenty-first century, we already see much new data and many perspectives suggestive of a burgeoning new worldview, not so much in the peer-reviewed mainstream (hypersensitive to 'reputation') but more in independent books. These things take a century or two; at the end of the nineteenth century, the universe seemed a simple clockwork mechanism, needing only to measure the rules better. This worldview of materialist science remains the norm among non-physicist scientists. However, (some) physicists are currently in a quandary, exemplified by the 100-year-old QM problem: does consciousness really influence the wave behaviour of subatomic particles? This question was sketched out elsewhere [1] and in Chapter 1.

This chapter is mainly addressed to fellow scientists who are more likely to stay with a materialist paradigm than the general public [2]. Although they may not realise it, they have a leadership responsibility to the general public on scientific issues that matter. The basic make-up of the universe matters to everyone in it. Although there are many more that show Sgt Willis' divide as clearly, I propose to look for reasons for it in the science of the following three numbered headings.

One more point: as scientists, we know that no explanation is currently final and, no matter how well documented, it is always subject to new data – the evidence is always key. Often, we must accept as our working hypothesis, an idea that seems most likely, provided no good data convincingly contradict it. The essences of the following are (for me) overwhelmingly the most likely explanations, which is why I present them here.

1. DEBUNKERS DEBUNKED

We are indebted to Robert McLuhan [3] for a detailed, even exhaustive, analysis of the committed debunkers of non-materialist ideas. He is well qualified, having the accolade of a page on RationalWiki, where he is described as a British promoter of pseudoscience unencumbered by formal science training and (horrors!) a council member of the Society for Psychical Research.

Here we need some explanation. Scientists are professional sceptics and, if necessary, debunkers; they are trained to look critically at and call out a new idea within their expertise, especially if it contradicts an established paradigm. Leiter [4] expresses a fascination with the psychology of the committed debunkers, the nihilists. He often finds they have a very early forced imposition of a faith-based philosophy, usually conventional religion, later fiercely rejected, 'vowing at a soul level never to be fooled again'. They gravitate to what seems the ultimate 'real' philosophy, science, unfortunately with a closed mind and believing science and only science has all the answers (scientism). Such psychologically scarred people may join sceptics organisations much as one might join any other support group, say Alcoholics Anonymous. There, they find comfort and consolation, with ridicule and ad hominem criticism of outsiders, playing to their own gallery. This fits self-confessed atheist and sceptic Richard Dawkins like a glove.

'Randi's Prize' was a million dollar offer by the professional trickster and stage magician James Randi to anyone who could convince him of the existence of the paranormal (psi), and the fact that no-one had claimed it was held as proof that psi does not exist! Self-importance on a pedestal. McLuhan describes his own journey as one seriously trying to understand the truth of psi reports because of their spiritual implications, which he considers do matter. He starts by examining the opinions of sceptics on 'irrational beliefs', and slowly comes to realise the superficial and invective-laden, even vicious and spiteful, nature of their statements. It is doubtful if any sceptics have ever read the original formal reports; McLuhan found a treasure-trove at the library of the Society for Psychical Research in West London and spent many hours doing just that. He also came to realise that psi was a very young science that had much to learn, especially making its experimental results proof against fraud – of which it was constantly accused, far beyond most sciences. Another realisation was that people vary enormously, even daily, similarly affecting replicability (as biologists know well). However, he also found that the researchers were always driven by curiosity, and had no material, religious or public relations opportunity for gain. They could be more critical than the sceptics, and claims were 'picked apart in forensic detail, with a detached and often sceptical spirit'.

McLuhan further explores specific areas of psi; firstly, as useful, detailed examples of poltergeist phenomena and the volatile but gifted Italian medium Eusapia Palladino. Clear instances of deception and fraud were found but were exceeded by genuinely unexplainable events. A more general survey of most areas of psi follows. More revealing for our present enquiry is the behaviour of the sceptics, especially Randi's, whose zeal is commendable, but one must ask: why? Curiosity was hardly a motive since he was only interested in possible areas of attack, not the truth, as it was 'obviously' all a lie.

Some reasons given for scepticism are also germane. Some are obviously not valid: 'surely mental effects must be confined to the brain'. Any argument 'surely' presupposes its weakness. Other reasons are obvious and valid: no tangible entity is proposed, only that 'something odd is going on', and most research is directed at proving that unlikely fact. Just so; this is an entirely new science and an exciting one. The observations have been endlessly replicated, but mentation is dependent on mental state (see whether chess masters can replicate their computer chess scores in a modern disco). Clearly a new theory of everything is needed.

Some reasons are spurious: accusations of 'New Ageism' and creationism, of deliberate cheating and its improbability on the scale needed. However, some points were well taken: security against fraud or the transmission of clues or hints; proper randomisation; the 'file drawer effect', where only

The Answer: Purpose (naturally)

desirable results might be selected for publication. When these objections were met, the interesting results persisted. The sceptics then changed tack: the aim became to create doubt by derision and emotive or abusive language. By this time, mainstream science had lost interest. McLuhan's book is an easy and fascinating read, although, at 800 pages, a shorter version may be timely.

Here, we may consider the contrast between the silver chain and the faggot ('faggot', a bundle of sticks; alternatively, the fasces symbol of collective strength of the ancient Roman republic, both terms uncomfortable). Most philosophical arguments comprise silver chains of syllogisms or other reasoning where the whole chain is no stronger than its weakest link. More scientifically, these are arguments in parallel (faggots) or in series (chains) where, respectively, a failure in one is irrelevant or catastrophic to the whole. It is surprising how many valid observations are consistently dismissed as merely 'anecdotal': how many anecdotes make a faggot? And how many airflights must you take before conceding that heavier-than-air flight is not impossible?

The late Victor Stenger PhD, a prolific and influential writer of nihilist books, was also an astrophysicist, emeritus professor of physics and astronomy (University of Hawai'i) and adjunct professor of philosophy (U. Colorado). Meaningfully, he was also a fellow of the Committee for the Scientific Investigation of Claims of the Paranormal, the top body of American sceptics. His book [5] really takes us into broader territory, and I will return to it in the end section. However, he presented as a more sophisticated sceptic, and so should his scientific arguments.

But I find he actually makes a series of quite ridiculous claims. Firstly, he dismisses all the data about extrasensory perception on the grounds that they do not meet the same criteria accepted by other sciences with an 'unbroken history of negative results'. That is simply untrue and means he has not actually read any original report, let alone all of them. He ignores the criteria standard in biology. He also states that 'extraordinary' claims need extraordinary evidence, but such claims only seem extraordinary to those with no personal or family experience of them. He regards meta-analysis as 'highly questionable' but does not explain why.

Then follows the most risible red herring of all. He states that when the *p* value is < 0.05, then 1 in 20 of the reports is wrong, and that all medical reports have this flaw! But what does 'wrong' mean? Using an imaginary test (say, the lengths of real herrings in a day's catch), it is not hard to assemble a series of 20 numbers to give a reasonable bell-shaped curve, a *p* value of 0.045 and a mean of 100.02 mm; the greatest deviation was 0.8 mm in two fish, above *and* below 100.00 mm, which average actually came up in only three fish. (This is a contrived experiment but quite an unsurprising outcome.) So which is the 'wrong' result? Clearly, this is a fallacious concept, which surely the author must have realised. His arguments against psi look more like expostulations, which vanish against the relative strength of the experimental evidence, where the faggot/fasces comprise so many independent observations that its overall strength is not compromised by weakness in one of them.

Finally, Stenger asks why psi has not caught on with mainstream science and concludes, therefore, that psi 'very likely does not exist'. He does not ask why so many bona fide scientists have persisted for 150 years with a science that seemingly does not exist. Stenger has illustrated Leiter's point perfectly.

2. THE TURIN SHROUD

How would you feel, dear reader, if you realised the Turin Shroud might be authentic after all? Oh no, not that sorry old chestnut you may say! And who would blame you – surely the cold water of the 1989 carbon dating [6] put out that old ember? However, recently, I read the original data for myself and noticed a curious anomaly.

Four contiguous samples were carefully cut from one edge of the shroud, and a portion of each was sent to three reliable labs for testing (Swiss Federal Institute of Technology at Zurich, U. Arizona at Tucson and Oxford University), together with three linen controls of age known from historical dating. The samples were cleaned using ultrasonic baths and several different textile methods (which did not affect the results), converted via carbon dioxide to graphite, then the $^{14}C/^{13}C$ ratios were measured by accelerator mass spectroscopy (AMS) and the $^{13}C/^{12}C$ ratios by conventional mass spectroscopy (Tucson and Oxford University). Zurich determined both $^{14}C/^{13}C$ and $^{13}C/^{12}C$ quasi-simultaneously by AMS. The operation was certificated, samples disbursed and results analysed statistically by The British Museum. The data were calibrated using known isotope ratios obtained by dendrochronological dating, and 3–5 replicate mass spectroscopy or AMS runs were performed on each sample. The control sample data are stated to agree well with previous radiocarbon and/or historical data but are not presented.

This is clearly rigorous science, and the results are summarised in Table 1.

Table 1. Radiocarbon dating of the Turin Shroud. [6]

Institution	Sample 1	Sample 2	Sample 3	Sample 4
Tucson	1304 ± 31	1023 ± 32	45 ± 46	1229 ± 43
Oxford	1200 ± 30	1010 ± 30	30 ± 35	1195 ± 30
Zurich	1274 ± 24	1009 ± 23	10 ± 30	1265 ± 34
Weighted means	**1261 ± 16**	**1013 ± 16**	**14 ± 20**	**1266 ± 20**

The values are expressed in years, AD or CE; the ranges are 68% confidence limits.

The use of the term 'radiocarbon dating', the collective prestige of the sponsoring institutions, the 21 authors and the publishing vehicle seem overwhelmingly impressive. But are they really?

These carefully obtained results on most precious materials appear to have been treated in an egregiously unscientific manner. While the three laboratories agree closely on each sample, the unanimous outlier of sample 3 (which also agrees well with conventional radiocarbon dating additionally done by The British Museum) is omitted, and the three other means are lumped together to yield a 'rounded calendar age of AD 1260-1390 with at least 95% confidence limits. This is held to be 'conclusive evidence that the linen of the Turin Shroud is mediaeval'! Such an incredible conclusion ignores the fact that replicates from each laboratory vary much less than the means among most samples, so the latter variation cannot be due to measurement error. There was no discussion of this conclusion in the paper, just this blunt statement. Ironically, sample 3 gives exactly the value expected if the shroud were authentic.

I could not have got away with this blatant fudging of an obvious sampling error in high school science, let alone a published paper. As a reviewer and editor, I would have felt obliged to demand resampling or outright rejection. I have not seen this aspect discussed elsewhere; was this a deliberate cover-up? If so, it seems they got away with it. If regarded as a simple undergraduate assay of four or 12 replicates, the means are, respectively, 888.5 AD and 882.8 AD, with standard deviations of 67% and 59.5% of the means, a very unimpressive assay. Reading the final results carefully, it is clear that sample 3 has been dismissed as an irrelevant outlier and only samples 1, 2 and 4 used, but I cannot find this explicitly stated. After this apparently surreptitious ploy, the results were further rounded *up* for technical reasons that are not quite clear. Contamination surviving the washings can only increase the apparent age towards modern values, so any suspicion should fall on the 'younger' ages given. What if all these three were the actual outliers? It seems the results were selected to support the 'rational' expectation. Wikipedia still records the shroud as mediaeval in April 2022.

The predictable result is that this extraordinary relic is written out of mainstream science. However, careful study has continued prolifically, necessarily in lower profile publications [7]. Dating by other less-accurate methods (opto-chemical and several mechanical methods [8]) show that the shroud fibres are certainly pre-medieval (90 AD ± 200 years, 95% confidence level). Scholars will always seek corroboration elsewhere regardless of whether doubt exists and may prefer to rely on historical/archaeological dating, for example, peat bog stratification or the Egyptian Pharaoh succession known from much fieldwork. The historical provenance of the shroud is incomplete, although credible, while archaeological evidence is very persuasive if not conclusive. The forensic pollen trail leads back to Constantinople, Urfa, in south-eastern Turkey near Syria (ancient Edessa, an important Christian centre of pilgrimage before the Saracen conquest) and Palestine in the Spring, while traces of soil found on the feet, knee regions, chest and face indicate an undefended, heavy fall in an area of aragonite travertine sand found around Jerusalem but rarely elsewhere. Edessa is associated with the Mandylion, a traditional cloth image of the face of Jesus said to be copied in some Byzantine coinage and many icons. The 3-D negative images (of unknown causation) on the shroud strikingly resemble these copies and are the most compelling evidence. They correspond exactly to the multiple traumas recorded as inflicted upon the historical Jesus [9,10]. Images on the eyelids could (debatably) be related to rare coin types issued during Pilate's governorship. The controversy has continued unresolved online but with vigour. At best, the 1988 data are misleading, even suspiciously so.

The buck naturally stopped with the then editor, the late Sir John Maddox, an occasional associate of James Randi. Why did he block this obvious debate?

Anyway, does this whole issue matter? Well, yes – profoundly. The images of the shroud, if authentic, would amount to a photographic record of the physical atrocities accepted by the voluntary Messenger to emphasise his vital message of the way the universe is comprised, not to mention a 3-D portrait of the Messenger himself. The unknown mechanism of image formation, certainly not man-made, could conceivably relate to a mechanism of resurrection. The public relations implications of this are enormous, more for the neutral observer than the committed Christian; its suppression quashes an important opportunity to reconcile some differences between religion and science. The key issue here is the nature of the universe: is it crucially non-material, as the Messenger insisted? We should watch that space.

3. REINCARNATION

If there exists a discarnate transferable package of all the skills, desires, foibles, memories and personality of a human individual that survives its death, then a reasonable place to look for one would be the presumably blank slate of a young child just learning to talk and express itself. In fact, posting one apparently successful find on Facebook elicited thousands of confirming responses; dozens of them are detailed [11]. These are not collectively convincing but far more than just persuasive – precisely the data to tempt a curiosity-driven study. This is actually how science progresses.

The late Ian Stevenson MD (professor of psychiatry at the University of Virginia) had, with colleagues, already famously applied such an approach; his scholarly works make slow reading for the layman, but shorter versions are now available [12, 13]. They offer a formidable portfolio of over

2500 carefully researched cases in which many have been independently verified and apparent previous lives identified ('solved' cases). Such memories may be linked with violent or otherwise especially memorable deaths, sometimes associated with birthmarks corresponding to death injuries. Reading case after case, corroborating detail after detail, leaves a feeling of no alternative to the reality of reincarnation in these cases.

Is this scientific proof of principle? Well, no; the concept is probably neither provable nor falsifiable yet as amenable for study by careful scientific methods as psychology and psychiatry, history and detective work [14]. Such data are certainly very persuasive – we have free choice as to whether we think the idea impossible or not. The question is also open as to whether all lifetimes are necessarily repeats.

Sceptics naturally have copious views here, and it is useful to understand them. McLuhan [3] reports many, which he considers in careful detail but leaves none with any substance, although he also reports many weaknesses in the data. Personally, I find his analysis compelling. However, Stenger is almost silent on the topic; he equates nirvana with nothingness. Such is the faith of nihilism.

It is not surprising that most cases of reincarnation are from Eastern countries where such belief is common, but a substantial number of Western presumptive cases have also come to light [13,15], some of them 'solved'. Two of the most persuasive are recent American cases [16,17] where in each case, while both parents were initially sceptical, one parent had severe emotional stress because of religious prohibitions. This would naturally reduce the incidence of reported cases, reinforced by ridicule from others, sometimes with almost medieval superstitious fear. Significantly, surviving shipmates/ teammates of the previous personalities seemed happy with their reincarnation as these little boys.

Why is there so much non-acceptance in the West? Belief in reincarnation is banned in Christianity and Islam: but why?

To quote American publisher and theosophist James M Pryse [18], 'while belief in reincarnation was almost universal in the time of Jesus and was an essential doctrine in all the so-called pagan religions, it is nowhere denied, disputed or questioned in the New Testament'. Indeed, several passages in the New Testament and the Old Testament are most reasonably interpreted to actually affirm it: it was not so much taught as just taken for granted then. So, what changed?

In his fascinating book on hypnotic past-life regressions with one unusual subject, Weiss [19] states that Constantine the Great and his mother the empress Helena edited out all reference to reincarnation, although this is contradicted by the few instances remaining. This idea was vigorously disputed online (resource no longer available) as lacking any reputable source. The most likely explanation is that by the sixth century AD, the Christian church had developed several teachings by earlier Church Fathers that were attracting away members and weakening the central church. At the 5th Ecumenical Congress of Constantinople (553 AD), such teachings were accordingly declared anathema and heresies. Unfortunately for future proper spiritual understanding, some (notably those of Origen) also included teaching of reincarnation. Apparently, belief in reincarnation was banned accidentally for political not spiritual issues!

There were other political problems. Ordinary people were being told that they were gods, with the promise of a life everlasting if they could just believe what the Messenger Jesus said; the bishops realised that, given their lack of sophistication, something stronger than just belief was needed. The ideas of a soul, a higher deity and Jesus were reconciled by the concept of the Holy Trinity in which Jesus was deified (an arguable blasphemy), but a concept familiar to Romans. The ancient pagan concepts of purgatory, limbo and hellfire were retained, presumably for extra discipline, and still remain, although they are not mentioned in the New Testament. These continue as problems for modern pilgrims trying to reconcile old religion with unconditional love.

The corollary of Stevenson's working hypothesis (see the first paragraph of this section) is that if the evidence for reincarnation is persuasive for you, then so it must be for the existence of that package of personality hypothetically surviving physical death. This is a most crucial acceptance. Several sincere Christians accept the likelihood of reincarnation. Perhaps, since the political pressure is gone, it is time for Western and Islamic churches to embrace this new spiritual opportunity.

THE 'WHY' QUESTION

We know our children are beginning to reason when the relentless 'why' questions start: this question presupposes some purpose to everything (and also that parents have the answers). We know that dogs are intelligent and can solve some problems by reason, especially if their genes are closer to wild type. We also find that dogs often query their pack leaders or owners; usually, the question is the 'I want' one, and sometimes 'how'. But without incentives in view (fun, food, fear), the 'why' question was not even on the menu for our five live-in companions over the years. So, can it be that the cosmic importance of the ultimate 'why' question does just not occur to nihilists? Or do they just fear the answer?

It seems that Sgt Willis' divide is alive and well outside politics. One illuminating outcome of the psi guessing games was that some participants consistently scored high while others scored low ('separating sheep and goats'); this seemed to correlate with confidence in their ability (i.e., whether they believed in it or not). 'Belief' or 'faith' can be a nebulous concept – at its core is really 'trust'. What or whom do you trust?

Stenger [5] uses many philosophical arguments in his denial of a non-material Mind. Personally, I found none remotely even gave me pause, but I have no qualification in philosophy, only the natural sort (PhD). Nevertheless, his entire case collapses on the basic premise of logic that a negative proposition can never be proved. One can only say that Stenger looked (and looked) for proof to convince *him* of a creative Mind and found none. Although he acknowledges the possibility of a hidden deity, he 'wants nothing to do with it' [5] (p. 240) but still does not bother to ask why such an entity might prefer to remain so.

Among the sceptics, we see scholars and scoffers, seekers and sneerers, doers and deniers. Their motivation also merits the 'why' question asked in each of the numbered sections above. For Randi and Stenger, balanced objectivity and the truth are clearly not in view; rather, they are like counsel for the prosecution trying to dazzle with part of the science and denying the rest to distract the jury – their object is only to win or appear to. Sometimes the invective becomes a little shrill and sounds like fear, which is interesting for the psychologist. Stenger has devoted at least six books to his thesis. Why? The lady doth protest too much, methinks.

CONCLUSIONS

Ours is a very young, self-aware species. If the history of the Earth were spread over a full calendar year, the first life (bacteria) appears in early February, the first dinosaurs appear by 10 December and leave on 25 December, the first *Homo* species appears by 11.45 pm, 31 December and the recorded history of humanity fills just the last minute [21]. Our species' immaturity is self-evident; like a 2–5-year-old in a tantrum, we *will not* share our toys or cake, and we will lash out at everybody in our way and even wreck the living room and everyone in it to get more cake. But we are getting bigger and more powerful; the living room soon will not cope unless we grow up a bit.

Also like your youngster, you cannot *make* her walk, but she will anyway (then your life will never be the same again).

But watch his face when he finally lets go of that table leg and steps out *alone*: surprise and triumph! She really wanted to do that; she knew she was human and wanted to move about upright like other humans. He trusted his ability and finally took that leap of faith. I remember that learning to swim was much the same.

I had long thought that word in the Anglican burial service was something of an oxymoron: how could there be a 'sure and certain *hope* of anything? I now realise that the Messengers could only tell us that a life everlasting existed, and even if we trusted them, we cannot *know* until we go there because we have been programmed largely to forget where we have already been. But, in a hopeless epoch, it was this hope that was the exciting new message.

If an omnipotent One Mind could create an entire universe, it could also emblazon all the heavens with an unambiguous symbol; then all humanity would fall to the ground in fear and be converted. Obvious and incontrovertible proof would amount to the same thing. However, this is not how an unconditionally loving parent would have it, consistent with absolute free will. Such a parent yearns for a child to *want* to love them back, a teacher aims for their student to *desire* to learn. Walsch [22] suggests a feasible understanding of how unconditional love can work in relation to the argument from evil.

Coercion of any kind is quite counterproductive. 'House rules' are different: children soon learn what works and what does not, like hot stoves. Karma can be likened to house rules spread over many lifetimes. Any action automatically gets its due reaction; no judgement is involved. We all yearn for our children to love us spontaneously, which they will if we show we love them back and can be trusted. All they, and humanity in relation to the One Mind, need to do is to take that small leap of trust and hope. We cannot expect ever to find firm scientific proof of purpose; all we are given are hints, such as the iceberg tips outlined above, available to us if we look with an open mind. Such approaches are anathema to the pure materialist; perhaps 'hope' is the difference between sheep and goats and the reason for Sgt Willis' divide. Many people live without ultimate hope and do not know it; much of this is due to scientists bamboozled by fearful debunkers.

REFERENCES

1. Cooper PD. A Real Fifth Dimension? *Explore.* 2017;13(1):62-67.
2. Gallup G. Jr. with Proctor W, quoted in Stevenson, ref 11 below, "67% of the general public believe in life after death, only 16% of scientists do". *Adventures in Immortality.* New York: McGraw-Hill, 1982.
3. McLuhan R. *Randi's Prize: What Sceptics Say About The Paranormal, Why They Are Wrong And Why It Matters.* Leicester UK: Matador Troubador, 2010.
4. Leiter LD. The Pathology of Organized Skepticism. J Sci Exploration, 16.(1):125–128, 2002.
5. Stenger VJ. *God: The Failed Hypothesis – How Science Shows That God Does Not Exist.* New York: Prometheus Books, 2008.
6. Damon PE and twenty others. Radiocarbon Dating Of The Shroud Of Turn. *Nature.* 337 1989 (6208) 611-615.
7. Fanti G and 23 others. Evidences for testing hypotheses about the body image formation of the Turin Shroud. 3rd Dallas Intl. Conf. on the Shroud of Turin. Dallas TX Sept 8-11. 2005.
8. Fanti G, Malfi P, Crosilla F. Mechanical And Opto-Chemical Dating Of The Turin Shroud. http://www.matec-conferences.org *Matec Web Of Conf.* 36, 01001. 2015.
9. Bevilacqua M, Fanti G, D'Arienzo M. The Causes of Jesus' Death in the Light of the Holy Bible and the Turin Shroud. Open J Trauma 1(2): 037-046. 2017.
10. Bevilacqua M, Fanti G, D'Arienzo M (2017) New Light on the Sufferings and the Burial of the Turin Shroud Man. Open J Trauma 1(2): 047-053. 2017.
11. Dyer WW, Garnes D. *Memories Of Heaven: Children's Astounding Recollections Of The Time Before They Came To Earth.* New York, NY: Hay House 2015.
12. Stevenson I. *Children Who Remember Previous Lives: A Question of Reincarnation. Revised ed.* Jefferson NC: McFarland and Co. Inc.: 2001.

13. Stevenson I. *European Cases of The Reincarnation Type.* Jefferson NC: McFarland and Co. Inc. 2003.
14. Wallace JW. *God's Crime Scene.* Colorado Springs, CO: David C Cook. 2015.
15. Harrison M, Harrison P. *Past Lives: Children Time Forgot.* Sinclair Publish. 2013.
16. Leininger B, Leininger A, Gross K. *Soul Survivor: The Reincarnation of a World War II Fighter Pilot.* 2009
17. Byrd C. *The Boy Who Knew Too Much.* New York, NY: Hay House Inc.; 2017.
18. Pryse JM. *Reincarnation in The New Testament.* Original ed. New York NY: Theosophical Soc. Publishing Dept.; 1904.
19. Weiss, BL. *Many lives, many masters.* New York NY: Simon & Schuster, Inc. 1988.
20. Eddy PR. http://www.focusonthefaulty.com/Pages/reincarnation.html
21. Ornstein R, Ehrlich P. *New World New Mind: Moving Toward Conscious Evolution.* New York: Doubleday. 1989.
22. Walsch ND. *God's Message To The World: You've Got Me All Wrong.* Faber VA: Rainbow Ridge Books LLC. 2014.

Chapter 5
The First Breakthrough

*__Shamanism thus constituted a major paradigm shift.
…it is easy to see how impressive such a revelation could be
in a small community…__*

Our Great Leap Forward and Us – Right Now

The flow'rs that bloom in the spring,
tra-la, have nothing to do with the case.
I've got to take under me wing, tra-la,
A most unattractive old thing, tra-la,
With a caricature of a face.

Ko-Ko, understandably declining Nanki-Poo's kind invitation to see the bright side of a lifetime with Katisha, The Mikado, W. S. Gilbert and A. Sullivan.

SUMMARY

Our universe lives with the paradox of closely guided chance, giving many billions of planets that could support life like ours. Life could not have arisen by chance, but once it started on Earth, we can trace its development as far as humans. Humans are genetically the 'third chimpanzee'. Evolution gave us more than just cleverness and a larger brain: it gave us emotional and, especially, spiritual intelligence. About 200,000–400,000 years ago, probably still in Africa, humanity made a great leap forward in the ability to innovate. The nature of this leap is still a mystery, but it led to greater adaptability and inventiveness and to the transition to the Upper Palaeolithic period. We suggest it lies in direct contact with the Universal Mind, the awareness of a non-material dimension including the soul, possibly via an NDE of an esteemed tribal elder reinforced by ongoing shamanic abilities. Shamanism and the ability to share with the Universal Mind constituted a major paradigm shift.

DNA studies show that most people leaving Africa went north into the Middle East, then Europe, Asia and the Far East, and on into North and then South America. But a smaller stream took a rapid southern beachcomber's route, via India, Southeast Asia and finally Australasia. All streams strongly retained their spiritual awareness and cultures.

First Nations Australians, the oldest undisturbed human culture outside Africa, provide rich sources of this history. A Universal Mind in which everyone is personally involved is everywhere understood, with an accepted law of respect and punishment. Sharing of resources was usual and group consciousness is shared in a form of meditation (Dreaming).

We stood face to face, barely three feet apart, the big adult male and I. Slightly taller, his arm span was twice mine and musculature probably four-fold. His jaws carried formidable weaponry and we both knew that in combat, I would last scarcely two seconds. Meeting his gaze for several seconds left me with a whiff of sullen dislike. Then, suddenly bored, he abruptly turned and ambled, on feet and knuckles, out of sight; my last glimpse was of his large testes, swinging free and unheeded. Naked and unaware.

Beside the two inches of toughened glass, what was it that separated us? Genetically, surprisingly little. He was a common chimpanzee, *Pan troglodytes*; with the closely related bonobo *Pan paniscus* our nearest living non-human relative. Molecular biology tells us our chromosomes overlap by 98.4% and, if judged by genealogical criteria usual for biological speciation, *Pan* and humans would be considered three species of the same genus. In fact, we are the third chimpanzee [1]. But we prefer to consider ourselves a separate genus, *Homo sapiens*, our extinct immediate forebears being *Homo erectus* and *Homo habilis*. Our brain size is 3–4 times greater than *Pan*'s although, more significantly, far more complexly interconnected. We are capable of far more complex thought, and, superficially, this seems the main effect of the seven million years of evolution between us. But there is probably something else, vastly more important. This is the focus of this chapter.

Albert Einstein once famously proclaimed that 'God does not play dice with the Universe', but, in fact, that is far from the truth. The universe is supremely orderly with rigid rules; it is the job of science to measure the rules very accurately to probe deeper rules. There is nothing disorderly about playing dice if each die is true and fair; it is actually extremely precise and predictable statistically, just a matter of throwing enough numbers at it. All chemical and subatomic reactions are affairs of chance involving very large numbers. A process of life essential to maintaining a healthy species and adapting to a changing environment –the reassortment of genes by fusion of haploid gametes – is a chance process where the odds may be shortened by various strategies.

Despite the ubiquity of randomness, the fact that we inhabit a universe whose physical rules are very closely defined (see Chapter 3) is wildly improbable by chance alone. Thus, we are faced with the apparent paradox of guided chance. According to the Big Bang theory (SC), less than 10^{19} seconds before the present time, some vast, primeval unknowable continuum was violently ripped apart at one tiny point so that the laws of chance following these rules resulted in a statistically predictable pattern of star and star cluster formation that allowed planets of all kinds to form. Some of these planets were sufficiently like ours where life like ours could develop. Such a universe has a beginning and, consequently, an end. Stars and planets would be true of any steady state theory, of course, and the SC can be shown to be quite unsafe in its fundamental assumptions [2] because each claimed support for the SC has a feasible alternative. If inertia is due to a Lorentz force resistance from the zero-point field [3], gravitational fields will always repel surrounding space and cause metric expansion of the universe. Dark energy would be simply gravitational inertia recoil. Expansion proceeds at a rate exactly matching insertion of protons (e.g., by gamma ray photofission). This leads to a novel steady state relation between entropy and gravity that drives maintenance and growth of the universe, as outlined in Chapter 1.

The stars are power plants that produce atoms of types defined by the rules, which life as we know it can use. Our galaxy alone probably contains more than 10^{11} planets like ours [4], and there are at least 2×10^{11} more galaxies in the visible universe – many potential homes for more life like ours. Given the amount of orderly thought needed to develop Earth and earthlings, it makes no sense that such great blueprints would not be adapted elsewhere where they fit.

Initiation of life on Earth also appears to be mindfully orchestrated. There has not been enough time or precursor materials to produce the incredible complexity of even the simplest life form by chance only (see Chapter 3), let alone the mysterious spark that ignites an inert mass of organic material to live, breathe and reproduce itself. The feasibility of panspermia ensures that life can be seeded to take advantage as soon as opportunity presents. All seems to be carefully engineered. It seems that this 'all' followed a purpose (see Chapter 4), hardly surprising given its scale.

The whole life chain of Earth – from bacteria, plants, vertebrates, dinosaurs, mammals to the great apes, including humans – can all be considered steppingstones to some end goal. Historians and scientists, including Diamond [1], argue that at some time in the last 200–100 kiloyears ago (kya, 1000 years ago), our recent ancestral *Homo sapiens* made a great leap forward. It is uncertain what exactly that was; Diamond suggests it was the use of language. However, that would entail copious changes in musculature, tongue and larynx combined with neurological development (i.e., in many genes) that are unlikely in such a short time, while many primates and great apes, even dogs, can use specific vocalisations or symbols to communicate specific ideas. Talking would certainly reinforce group memory and may be an essential prerequisite, but it does not explain non-material constructs like inventiveness, appreciation of art and decoration and the imagination for concepts of an afterlife and the supernatural. Above all, Klein and Edgar [5] highlight that it was a 'quantum advance in human ability to innovate that marks the dawn of human culture', with uniquely modern adaptability to change without bodily variation.

In another and deeply illuminating book, Diamond [6] revisits the great leap motif but again fails to identify its cause. He shows that the superior attainments of Western and Eurasian civilisations did not arise from superior abilities but from lucky combinations of cultivable foodstuffs on suitable lands and climates; easy East–West transit and sharing of inventive ideas; and large populations to develop disease resistance and support a privileged class with leisure to invent. The penalty was the frequent degradation of the environment, impelling expansion, removal or collapse.

Throughout the twentieth century, solid evidence has accumulated that the events hitherto assumed confined to neural networks within the human brain can exchange ideas or have physical effects non-locally outside it. Early in the twenty-first century, that evidence has reached the critical mass of absolutely no reasonable alternative (see Chapter 1). The ramifications of such certain science are so far-reaching as to be staggering. Certainly, doubters remain, but their reasons seem more a matter of disinterest or immovable faith than of logic (see Chapter 4). Taking one aspect, reincarnation, there seems no reasonable alternative to a discrete package of an entire personality analogous to a soul being transferred to a freshly minted human embryo in utero, sometimes complete with physical reminders of the previous personality's face or body and unnatural manner of death. This concept is quite ancient among humans.

The William James Legacy. Its origin presumably lies in the prehistory of religion, or at least in the evolution of a spiritual awareness sometimes termed the religious mind.

The First Breakthrough

Rossano [7] quotes William James (the founder with Frederic William Henry Myers of modern psychology) as arguing that religious experience (e.g., near-death, deathbed and out-of-body experiences) was the origin of religion, and accounts of many modern examples [8,9,10] make this idea very hard to discount. Minor instances of the last two occurred in my own recent family. Philosophers and scientists recognise people's need for religion, present various definitions of it [11] and may puzzle as materialists do over its cause or possible utility, confusing religion with spirituality. They note the soothing effect of prayer but seem unaware of the huge power of the 'sure knowing' in a religious experience both for the experiencer and their close community. One wonders how many people worldwide have pondered the last words (oh wow, oh wow, oh wow, addressed to an invisible third party) of the well-known late Steve Jobs [12].

Rossano [7] summarises the hypotheses of spiritual evolution in three stages. The first stage, the pre-Upper Palaeolithic era (300–150 kya), involved ecstatic altered-state rituals (whirling, group dancing, psychedelic drugs, etc.) that formed the social bonding essential for cohesive societies larger than family groups. The second stage, the Upper Palaeolithic era (after 150 kya), was characterised by the transition to shamanistic healing rituals, analogous to prayer groups. Shamanism may well be triggered by a James' 'holy instant', especially if this were due to a NDE [13]. It is easy to see how impressive such a revelation could be in a small community given the life-changing nature of such experiences, especially if involving an esteemed elder and if reinforced by repeated synchronicities and psychic events, such as the ability to prophesise.

In the third stage, the bright-red natural pigment red ochre – of no obvious utility to hunter-gatherers but, nevertheless, deliberately mined and 'not infrequently' carried many miles to African hominid sites (100–200 kya) [7] – may be an early indicator of religious ceremonies. The ochres were extensively mined and traded by hunter-gatherer groups and are still sacred to First Nations Australians. Cave art, ritualistic burials and artefacts give later evidence (30 kya) of sacred sites, prayer rituals and ancestor worship with the emergence of theological elites and complex narratives of the supernatural.

Rossano also correlates the first and second stages with the early development of human infants who, from 12 months on, seem to expect human actions to be purposeful (i.e., goal-directed from beliefs and desires). Such expectation has been argued as the critical cognitive distinction between apes and humans. In addition, animals, including some apes, appear very limited in their ability to recall personal history at will [7] (episodic memory) or to plan ahead. Non-human animals have limited development of their prefrontal cortex. This appears like humans less than four years old, correlating with complex development of the prefrontal cortex; hence, presumably, the Freudian insight of seeking the cause of adult psychoses in the inchoate memory of psychological trauma in early childhood. If episodic memory is of, for example, holy instances, and is interpreted by the novel concept of the supernatural, it may mark the emergence of shamanism.

It is still unclear whether the hugely significant human exodus from Africa occurred in a single wave or in many [14] and whether the main wave was 70–50 kya or 110–90 kya; severe bottlenecks limited the spread and, thus, genetic diversity, probably due to climatic factors. All models roughly overlap the shamanic transition into the Upper Palaeolithic after 150 kya, which almost certainly began in East Africa. Timelines can be provided by DNA studies (mitochondrial [mt], Y chromosome, certain autosomal genes or whole-of-genome) where the molecular clock of spontaneous mutation allows for the calculation of time separations of fossil finds (although mutation rates have varied), and hence of migration routes in prehistory.

When humans first left Africa, it seems from many studies that a mtDNA sub haplotype of M haplotypes termed 'N' took an unidentified northerly route, and its derived streams of mtDNA sub haplotypes have been traced into Europe, Asia and the Far East, and on into North and then South America. We know of the development of Eurasian and American civilisations with something of their associated belief systems. Awareness of the supernatural was universal and, unsurprisingly, was often associated with as-yet-occult but obvious natural phenomena (lightning, rainbows, the progressions of planets, sun and seasons). Each separate event may be the responsibility of a given deity with human feelings, desires and behaviour. Ancient Egypt exemplified a focus on the afterlife. Pantheism was a natural consequence; Westerners still recall it in names for days and months. Until the advent of the Messengers (see Chapter 2), Western humanity did not seem to associate itself with the divine.

An mtDNA study in isolated, relict, aboriginal populations of Southeast Asia [15] has its problems but suggests only a single main dispersal of the M haplotype from the African side of the mouth of the Red Sea (~65 kya). The N sub haplotype of M possibly turned north from M, while M continued via a southern beachcomber's route, through India and onward into Southeast Asia and Australasia, most likely spreading rapidly within only a few thousand years.

The First Nations Australians' record keeping. First Nations Australians, in situ by at latest 65–60 kya [16], are importantly relevant here for at least three reasons. First, they are among the oldest continuous undisturbed human cultures outside Africa; they are still with us and have much to teach. Second, they are a very spiritual society with an extant and strong community ethos despite much damage since European settlement in 1788. Third, they have a robust traditional system for the preservation of origin myth, legend and tribal memory, in ritualised song, dance and artwork.

The stories may be the inherited memory of a significant event, such as among the Googanji/Yidiniji peoples near

Cairns in tropical Queensland [17], who regularly hold a song and dance ceremony to mark a time when a shallow sea invaded their food areas (the present Great Barrier Reef) at a rate up to 200 metres per year over a span of a single human lifetime. This forced repeated retreats eventually of 10–20 km and corresponds to the time of maximum thaw of the ice sheets, ca 10 kya. Flood folk memories are found around the Fertile Crescent, but the Cairns memory is unusual in its accurate location, which allows dating.

Regarding artwork, I once treasured a bark painting of the Dreamtime creation story *Wagilak sisters' story* [18], signed by the artist Dawidi Birritjama. It was his inherited duty to regularly sing and paint the story, often in a group setting with children, ensuring accurate group memory and a successor in line for all future time. Like the Buddhist monks' chanted sand mandalas [19] – and indeed familiar religious ceremonies (Christian Easter, Jewish Passover) – the sole objective is to consciously remember significant history; any material product is superfluous. The many Australian Dreamtime stories [20] illustrate sophisticated, complex spiritual cultures more accurately reproducible in detail than assumed likely in casual campfire storytelling. Significantly, one story is of the creation of a specific sacred site of the Wilyeru peoples of northern Flinders Ranges, South Australia, who made annual pilgrimages there for red ochre to use in their manhood initiation circumcision ceremonies. Was this the purpose of the African red ochre hominid sites 100–200 kya?

Although specific deities may cause natural phenomena, the main First Nations Australian theological concepts were quite simple and familiar: a discarnate spirit inhabits an earthly body until it wears out and then is ferried across a river to join ancestors before reincarnating. One may commune directly (Dream) with the aggregate of ancestral spirits without the need for an intermediary. This does not differ from modern religious practice, except for the absence of a nominated Messenger and priestly intermediary. A Universal Mind in which everyone is personally involved is everywhere understood, with accepted rules of respectful human behaviour towards others and an understood law and punishment for transgressors. Sharing of resources was usual in the tribe, and personal possessions were minimal.

The First Nations Australians managed a fragile environment well, particularly land conservation and the use of fire to keep land clear and refresh pasture. At the time of European arrival, the entire country was stably populated at low density with a homogeneous matriarchal society (97.7% speaking one of the Paman-Nyungan languages) and mtDNA haplotype M [21], with a strong affinity to 'Country' (local region) such that the Country owns the people rather than the usual Eurasian reverse. First Nations Australian law insisted that land was held in common, and humans were merely custodians. For better or for worse, life resources were too meagre for First Nations Australian peoples to gain the critical mass to develop advanced technology.

Ko-Ko's dilemma. What has Ko-Ko's dilemma (see the Prologue to this Chapter) and *Pan troglodytes* to do with all this history? I hope that their relevance to our story can help us understand how our long journey has left us in the following three current and linked situations.

1. Humanity presently has the collective wealth and know-how to make this entire planet a far safer, happier and fruitful place conducive to the quiet development and introspection we are bred for. However, we fail to make it so because we have fear, the real antithesis of love. We fear war; lack of money; non-productive, forced idleness; loneliness; ill health and death; dispossession and subjugation; and even a political system allowing wider sharing. The concept of 'enough' is rare in personal or corporate wealth. Fear is predictable in this world.

2. If humanity arose with a purpose, then we surely have far to go. The One Mind, inclusive of humanity, is synonymous with love and is not pantheistic. Here we see the role of the Messengers (see Chapter 2), whose unanimous intent was to remind us of that truth and of our part in it. Humanity's purpose may be simply to trust the One Mind [22], of which we are, in essence, just a part. Our job is to remember, consciously and always, that truth and learn mindfully, over however many lifetimes it may take, how to behave to take our eventual place in the One Mind.
3. We are presently like poor Ko-Ko, knowing what he must do but not yet trusting enough to risk it. If we dislike the idea that our short-lived earthly forms are selectively bred merely as vehicles for serial lifetimes of essence schooling, we can reflect on *Pan troglodytes* to understand the huge privilege of being *Pan tertius*, aka *Homo* nearly-*sapiens*, and the joys and duties entailed. Somehow our human brain has been evolved and engineered like a television set, a rare receptor for sprigs of the One Mind, and we are still learning how to tune it. Other species apparently differ. These sprigs are somehow also us. For this, we can be grateful.

Perhaps it is now time on Earth for another great leap; perhaps also it needs to be done mindfully (i.e., *consciously*), and perhaps we already know how to do it (see Chapter 1).

Recently [23], some 15,000 people were internet-guided to direct a Peace Intention to the Sri Lankan war zone in 10-minute synchronised bursts at specific times. Peace did rapidly come about but may have resulted from normal ground conditions. The unexpected finding was that thousands of participants themselves spontaneously reported strange experiences: 'total integration into the whole', a 'divine order', universal connectedness, purpose not random, something greater than oneself with its own healing power, often weeping or sobbing with joy, not sorrow – a kind of mirror healing effect. Groups as small as eight have shown benefit *within* the group, provided the intention is directed *outside* the group. As mentioned in the first section of this book, I had a similar experience. The surest path to Wisdom is experiential (see Chapter 6). These are varieties of religious experience.

Behaviour can evolve and spread much faster than molecular genetic change. An idea is 'catching' and can spread indefinitely without destroying its substrate – a song, a joke, a theoretical abstract. However, it must be understandable in the current paradigm, directly or by metaphor, allegory or analogy. Psi and the supernatural cannot be understood in a purely materialist paradigm, while late–Stone Age peoples were strongly aware of a non-material dimension. *Shamanism thus constituted a major paradigm shift.*

This shift, corresponding with [7] or even causing the transition to the Upper Palaeolithic (after 150 kya), seems the strongest candidate for any great leap. Clearly, an effective resident healer would improve the survival of the village and its neighbours, while access to the wisdom of the One Mind should speed-up innovation. How many creative people believe their ideas came solely from themselves or can discount any strange 'coincidences' along the way? Such experience may change the world, but, primarily, it changes us. This may be a key: our change seems to radiate change.

McTaggart's experiment opens an exciting prospect for the twenty-first century. What makes it special is that we can, perhaps, see our great leap coming to flower before our eyes, *right now.* (Maybe we are not yet ready for any fruit.) Where can such a privilege take us all?

For Barbara 2014, and for David 2017.

REFERENCES

1. Diamond J. *The Third Chimpanzee: The Evolution and Future of the Human Animal.* New York: Harper Collins; 1991.
2. Cooper, PD. A Steady State Better Explains a Metrically Expanding Universe and the Vital Interplay of Entropy and Gravity. *Intl J Astrobiol Aerospace Technol.* 2019; 02: 107. DOI: 10.29011/IJAAT-107.100007
   httpps://gavinpublishers.com/assets/articles_pdf/1570626126 article_pdf18065791.pdf
3. Haisch B, Rueda A, Puthoff HE Inertia as a Zero-Point-Field Lorentz force. *Phys. Rev. A.* 1994; 49 678-694.
4. www.nasa.gov/kepler
5. Klein RG, Edgar B. *The Dawn of Human Culture.* New York: John Wiley, 2002.
6. Diamond J. *Guns, Germs and Steel.* London: Vintage Books, 1998.
7. Rossano MJ. The Religious Mind and the Evolution of Religion. *Rev. Gen. Psychol.* 2006; 10(4): 46-364.
8. Alexander E. *Proof of Heaven. A neurosurgeon's journey into the afterlife.* Sydney: Pan Macmillan Australia; 2012.
9. Ritchie GG, Sherrill E. *Return from Tomorrow.* Grand Rapids MI: Chosen; 2007.
10. Barbato M. *Reflections of a Setting Sun: Healing experiences around death.* 2nd edn. Adelaide, South Australia: Griffin Press, 2016.
11. Dawkins R. *The God Delusion.* London UK: Transworld Publishers; 2006.
12. Steve Jobs's last words www.theguardian.com/
13. Ring K. 1985. *Heading Toward Omega: in Search of the Meaning of the Near-Death Experience.* Amazon Kindle Books.
14. López S, van Dorp L, Hellenthal, G. Human Dispersal Out of Africa: A Lasting Debate. *Bioinform Online.* 2015; 11(2): 57–68. Online 2016 Apr 21. doi: 10.4137/EBO.S3348
15. Macaulay V et al. Single, Rapid Coastal Settlement of Asia Revealed by Analysis of Complete Mitochondrial Genomes. *Science* 2005; 308(5724): 1034-1036.
16. http://www.abc.net.au/news/science/2017-07-20/aboriginal-sheltehuman-history-back-to-65,000-years/8719314
17. Reid N, Nunn P, Shape M. Indigenous Australian stories and sea level change. *Proc. 18th Conf. Foundation for Endangered Languages,* 2014; 82-87.

18. Wagilak sisters' story https://www.artgallery.nsw.gov.au/collection/works/IA45.1960
19. Buddhist sand mandalas. https://commons.wikimedia.org/wiki/File%3AChenrezig_Sand_Mandala.jpg
20. Roberts A. *Dreamtime: the Aboriginal Heritage.* Superb interpretive artwork and references here and others in Roberts' Dreamtime Series. Adelaide, South Australia: Rigby Publishers Ltd; 1981.
21. Nagel N et al. Aboriginal Australian mitochondrial genome variation – an increased understanding of population antiquity and diversity. *Nature Publishing Group Sci. Rep.* 2017; 7:43041. https://www.researchgate.net/publication/314982192
22. Dossey L. *One Mind. How our Individual Mind is part of a Greater Consciousness and Why it Matters.* Carlsbad, CA: Hay House; 2013.
23. McTaggart L. *The Power of Eight: Harnessing the Miraculous Energies of a Small Group to Heal Others, Your Life and the World.* London UK: Hay House; 2017.

Chapter 6
Humanity's Achilles' Heel

Intuitive Mind is a sacred gift, Rational Mind its faithful servant.
We now often worship the servant and deride the divine.
Bob Samples, 1976,
interpreting the views of Albert Einstein

Quo Vadis, Human Intuitive Mind?

SUMMARY

This chapter is about the enigma of the human personality and how it relates to the universe in which we live. It is possibly the heart of this book and the reason it came into being. Iain McGilchrist's *The Master and His Emissary* [1,2] is a useful starting point. It collates 30 years of work that shows how our left (rational) and right (intuitive) brain hemispheres work together. The Big Five (OCEAN) personality test reveals some disturbing truths suggestive of humanity's dark side but fails to specifically include intuition. Conversely, the well-known yet controversial Myers-Briggs Personality Score specifically includes intuition and shows intuition's importance to at least one-third of normal people, with possibly a gradation in intuitive thinking. Intuition implies immediate knowing without words, a non-verbal communication practised by one group of First Nations Australians. Vociferous reaction against psi and the paranormal ('pseudoscience') is clearly dominated by the left brain. Current human predicaments are shown to be due to the dominance of left-brain thinking: in world politics, the battle between good and evil, the battle for Earth's climate, the battle for human survival. The divided brain may provide a physical basis for the Satan concept. The collective human psyche may be journeying towards right–left balance; in short supply now is respect and right-brain thinking.

In an online video on his massive 20-year study *The Master and His Emissary: The Divided Brain and the Making of the Western World* [1,2], the psychiatrist and English literature Oxford don Iain McGilchrist wished he had seen the quotation of Albert Einstein before he started his study. Had he done so, our understanding might well have been the poorer; his hard work means that Einstein's insight has a basis of solid evidence and independent verification. His study, analysing a formidable bibliography 'often using very particular accidents of nature, or carefully contrived artificial experiments that highlight what otherwise goes unremarked', collated in one place the importance of the intuitive mind (right brain) in balancing the necessary action of the rational mind (left brain). The left brain on its own could easily misinterpret the entire point at issue. Much of the work of the corpus callosum, the physical bridge between the two halves of the brain, consists paradoxically in suppression, keeping the two halves apart and in ignorance of each other yet achieving balance, like the two hands of a concert pianist.

THE LEFT BRAIN – RIGHT BRAIN CONUNDRUM

McGilchrist's question comes from the known fact that, in all higher animals, the brain is divided into two hemispheres that are joined by the corpus callosum. This is dictated early in embryology and, hence, early in ontogeny generally. Why is such duplication of function so necessary in such an important and genetically expensive organ?

McGilchrist's key approach was to ask not what each half *did*, but rather what it was *like*: its values, goals, interests – how and why did it do what it did? How does each hemisphere engage with the world?

His answer can be summarised by the following personal anecdote:

> One morning, I was throwing breadcrumbs for our local and friendly male Australasian swamp hen (*Porphyrio melanotus*) who was running eagerly towards them (left brain engaged). Suddenly the resident male Australian magpie (*Gymnorhina tibicen*), who being highly territorial naturally owned any food on that patch. angrily swooped onto a nearby fence. But by the time he landed, the swamp hen was already in the air at the height of the fence, bill agape in defensive posture (right brain engaged).

We seek here to highlight, inter alia, the interplay of the intuitive mind with other personality traits in the light of McGilchrist's work and Einstein's insight.

THE BIG FIVE PERSONALITY TEST AND MCGILCHRIST'S DESIGNATIONS

Academic psychology prefers the Big Five (or OCEAN) method as the most rational approach to analysing general personality traits. These five traits are O (openness to new ideas/experiences), C (conscientiousness), E (extroversion), A (agreeableness) and N (emotional stability).

Some salient aspects of the character of each hemisphere are extracted from McGilchrist's analysis (see Table 2). They show patterns of thinking, which, if translated into habitual behaviour would be termed personality traits. By assuming extreme scores for each trait, one can assign 'personalities' to each numbered category in Table 2. Each trait is then evaluated by the OCEAN method (illustrated in italics in Table 2).

Table 2. Summary of McGilchrist's designations and the OCEAN Personality Test.

Left brain	Right brain
1. Narrow beam precisely focused on 'get and grasp'; most of language and meaning. *Low O. Low A. High C (discrimination).*	1. Sustains attention and vigilance on everything else; connects, explores, relations. *High O.*
2. Narrows things to a certainty. *Low O. High C.*	2. Open to possibilities. *High O.*
3. Tends to fixity (either/or) *Low O. High C.*	3. Tends to flow (both/and). *High O.*
4. Not reality, self-referring tokens. *Low C (fails to discriminate).*	4. Relations, betweenness. *High O. High C. High A.*

5. Destroys metaphor, jokes, poetry, music etc. by explaining them. *Low O. Low C.*	5. Understands and enjoys metaphor, jokes, poetry, music, etc. *High O. High A.*
6. Competitive; primary motivation is power. *High E. Low A.*	6. Seeks cooperation, harmony, balance. *High O. High A.*
7. Does not realise its own limitations. *Low O. Low C.*	7. Sometimes has doubts. *High O. High C.*
8. Uses logic to manipulate, persuade, seduce, or win, not to understand. *Low O. Low C. High E. Low A.* *This is the scientism method*	8. Uses logic to understand, often coupled with experience or experiment. *High O. High C. High A.* *This is the Scientific Method.*

Note: conclusions in italics.

To summarise Table 2, the left brain is:

- uniformly low in openness (O) (8/8)
- only high in conscientiousness (C) in language and meaning (3/8), otherwise often careless in discrimination (4/8)
- sometimes obtrusive in extroversion (E) (2/8)
- often low in agreeableness (A) (4/8).

The right brain is:

- uniformly high in openness (O) (8/8)
- generally high in conscientiousness (C) (7/8)
- often high in agreeableness (A) (4/8)
- always balanced in extroversion (E) (0/8).

My personal outstanding impressions from Table 2 are the defects in human character displayed by the left brain. I would not choose it as a friend and companion; however, it might be my choice for an enemy because of its low C scores. It would clearly be a useful servant if it were firmly under control. It would be a dangerous master.

In contrast, the right brain is almost angelic. Aside from the angel implication from scholarly philosophical intuition (see Section 'Where Else Does Intuition Serve' in this chapter), Intuition is not revealed in the OCEAN personality test unless, by omission, it is part of openness.

We do not see the personality trait N (emotional stability) displayed in Table 2.

THE MYERS-BRIGGS PERSONALITY TEST AND MCGILCHRIST'S DESIGNATIONS

The well-known and controversial Myers-Briggs personality test has been widely used by human resource personnel and has equally been widely criticised as a predictor of performance and happiness. Its popularity may only indicate better marketing. It is true that it only designates Jung-style stereotypes (people change and develop); the tests only use preferences rather than strict rules of behaviour. People rarely fit neatly into boxes and often seem to fit more than one. Nevertheless, the Myers-Briggs personality test specifically allows respondents to self-report the use of feeling or intuition, which the OCEAN method does not. This constitutes a significant failure of the OCEAN method, as intuition is an important feature of personality (as shown in Table 3) while openness only offers a hint. In fact, the academic opposition to the Myers-Briggs option, which seems the more intuitive, in preference to the OCEAN test may be considered a left-brain (rationalist) choice.

Here, I wish to refer to the preference choice criteria listed in the Wikipedia entry for the Myers-Briggs Type Indicator <https://en.wikipedia.org/wiki/Myers–Briggs Type Indicator>. (Many of the attempted editing issues affecting this website may reflect the left-brain dominated views raised by its allusion to intuition.) Considering these categories in light of the divided-brain analysis, I firstly regard the E/I (Extrovert/Introvert, Choice 1) and the J/P (Judging/Perceiving, Choice 4) invitations to be divided-brain neutral. But looking carefully at the S/N (Sensing/Intuition, Choice 2) and T/F (Thinking/Feeling, Choice 3) invitations, which ask you how you prefer to take in information and then make decisions on it, each question in effect asks you whether you prefer using Sensing/Thinking, S/T (your left brain?) or Intuition/Feeling, N/F (your right brain?) to pay attention.

I have rearranged the resulting combinations of E/I, S/N, T/F and J/P (see Table 3) to reflect the degree of inferred left brain – right brain orientation implied by the choices offered. The 'trade names' are derived from those of David Keirsey's Keirsey Temperament Sorter from the Wikipedia website.

Table 3. The sixteen Myers-Briggs types rearranged to reflect brain orientation.

Left brain		Right brain	
Rationalists	Guardians	Artisans	Idealists
INTP	ISTJ	ISTP	INFP
4.0	12.5	5.0	4.5
Diagnoser	*Inspector*	*Crafter*	*Healer*
INTJ	ISFJ	ISFP	INFJ
3.0	11.5	7.0	2.0
Organiser	*Protector*	*Nurturer*	*Counsellor*
ENTP	ESTJ	ESFP	ENFJ
3.5	10.0	6.5	3.5
Solver	*Supervisor*	*Performer*	*Teacher*
ENTJ	ESFJ	ESTP	ENFP
3.5	10.0	4.5	7.0
Field Marshall	*Provider*	*Promoter*	*Champion*

The numbers refer to the average proportion (percentage) of each type in the United States population as of about 2015 AD, from the Wikipedia entry.

Of the total, 14.0% are Rationalists, 44.0% are Guardians, 23.0% are Artisans and 17.0% are Idealists. Thus, 58.0% prefer the left brain and 40% prefer the right, showing a gradation in intuitiveness in the normal population reading from left to right in Table 3. While not the majority, we note that intuition/feeling is important to more than a third of the population studied, or if the scores for N and F are summed, 59.%.

WHERE ELSE DOES INTUITION SERVE?

The answer is 'probably everywhere else in life'. The Shorter Oxford Dictionary (3rd ed., 1973) shows several definitions for intuition. One, termed 'scholarly philosophical', is the immediate knowledge ascribed to angelic or spiritual beings with whom both vision and knowledge are identical. Another, termed 'modern philosophical', is the immediate apprehension of an object without the intervention of any reasoning process. Others include a power of the mind to perceive the truth of things without reasoning or analysis, a knowing without physical means and a non-material awareness. Immediacy is always crucial. Somehow, the intuitive mind seems able to merge with some universal awareness and instantly become aware. Many people associate intuition with psi, clairvoyance, etc., with good reason.

The essence here is communication. The development of speech and language has been recognised as a crucial breakthrough in human culture; however, this has taken many serial genetic modifications and possibly a million years of trial and error.

Intuition has yet another way, completely unambiguous and exemplified by some First Nations Australians (see Chapter 7). These people spend much time 'Dreaming', a form of meditation. One result of this practice is that people could and did routinely communicate non-verbally, telepathically. Here, communication becomes scholarly intuition as defined in the Shorter Oxford Dictionary.

There are at least two further important ways for intuition to help us. Emeritus Professor neuroscientist Marjorie Woollacott [3] received during regular meditation a religious experience, unforgettable in complete detail for a lifetime and very like my epiphany (see the start of this book). Fortunately, her background and her training in Eastern philosophy enable a more general appreciation. For example, James's and Myers's Filter Theory anticipates Peake's 'leaky reducing valve' concept in reducing the 'noise of genuine realities' (see Chapter 1, 'Illusions of the First Kind – The Five Senses Determinant').

Woollacott's book is an important and addictive read that covers the gamut of consciousness, even without a functioning brain. It is unsurprisingly firmly post-materialist and renders the mind–body problem a clear non-problem (brain does not cause Consciousness). As in the Prologue to the book you are reading, Woollacott found difficulty with materialism in fellow scientists; that is why I described my approach as naive, without prejudice.

Similarly, another important contribution, *Discerning Your God Self* by Bernard Bernstein [4], covers many of the topics outlined in this book, often with a different perspective. For example, 'Wisdom is Experiential': the 'Aha- light bulb apprehension' in a student's experience is his alone.

Bernstein's book describes itself as designed as a practical guide for seekers of spiritual wisdom; it is not an academic contribution. It is about spirituality, *not* religion; I have complained elsewhere in these pages (see Chapter 2) about this confusion.

Some terms used here overlap somewhat. Also, academic psychology is uncomfortable with the right–left brain dichotomy because of neuroplasticity and outdated argument. It seems more direct to collect McGilchrist's and Peake's into one and use Bernstein's concepts, referring to the God Self (right brain, Daemon) or the Ego Self (left brain, Eidolon).

The value of Woollacott's and Bernstein's books, and that of Eben Alexander (see Chapter 2) and Gary Holz (see Chapter 7) lies in their first-person accounts: they were experienced first-hand.

Philosophers have speculated that humanity's goal is to achieve a large-scale collective change in human consciousness before we ultimately destroy our planet [5,6], a transcendental shift, a deliberate focusing of intention on connecting to 'Mind at Large'. This is amplified in Chapter 1, in the Section 'Illusions of the Second Kind – the Quantum Determinant'.

It is almost as if the human intuitive mind, like a collective psyche of humanity, is on a journey. It is now at a fork in the road, which, because of its habit of repeatedly ignoring the needs of its home planet for non-essential material gain or pleasure, is near an apocalypse. McGilchrist's work makes the cause plain as the dominance of the servant, the left brain, over the master, the right brain, or the dominance of the Ego Self over the God Self. As at Vanity Fair, many people strive mightily for that which is not worth having.

DISCUSSION

The universe (material or non-material) being composed entirely of energy and consciousness, the only premise possible is that the universe is basically Mind-stuff (i.e., spiritual). All other properties must follow from that, even the illusions that earthlings must live in.

The opinions of the committed sceptics were 'like Counsel for the Prosecution, trying to dazzle with part of the Science and denying the rest to distract the jury; their object was only to win, or appear to'. This precisely fits our collected designation of the Ego Self's strategy.

In fact, the closeness of the behaviour of the organised sceptics regarding psi with Ego Self tactics is almost uncanny (see Table 2), including that of the famous sceptic Richard

Dawkins (see Chapter 2). The same is true of the almost desperate behaviour of James Randi, of Randi's Prize fame (see Chapter 4), which now becomes understandable. If scientism is equated with the Ego Self, then it follows that acceptance of soundly based psi experimental data should involve a degree of intuitive awareness of God Self (imagination?).

Thus, our collected explanations of the rational mind provide a satisfying explanation of the sceptics' behaviours, although they must be driven by a strong emotion. In each case, one gets a whiff of fear: fear of what? Part of the cause is the desperate activity of the sceptics themselves (see Chapter 4). Fear is catching and self-amplifying. Perhaps here is the display of emotional instability (N) missing from Table 2. Some vital but neglected forms of communication, which surely are activities of the intuitive mind, are grouped (see Chapter 1) as Illusions of the Second Kind. Examples of its relevance in our daily life are instances of sustained intention, synchronicity and the guardian angel.

The properties of the left brain – the Ego Self – described in Table 2 distressingly resemble current politicians' attitudes, of any flavour that I have observed: they must conform to survive. We clearly need better criteria for selecting our leaders. Among them, we can recognise Napoleon, Hitler, Stalin and certain others still in play. The current mindset of the Chinese Communist Party in 're-educating' its Muslim minority displays a total ideological ignorance of humanity's urge to reunite with its spiritual roots. To the Ego Self, a spiritual universe is a contradiction in terms and just cannot be.

McGilchrist also sketches the types of society that would result from the rigorous application of Ego Self ideology; among these, we see familiar dystopian scenarios, such as *Brave New World* (Aldous Huxley), *1984* and *Animal Farm* (George Orwell). C.S. Lewis used a different premise in his Narnia series for children and *The Space Trilogy* for adults, that of the battle between good and evil.

The Satan concept is a feature of the Abrahamic religions but appears to have counterparts in other spiritual thought as devils or demons. Sometimes, they are personified but more often used as metaphors for an inclination or choice among the many choices we face as material beings.

The key question is posed: does the left hemisphere – Ego Self – represent the dark side of human nature, with which we must forever contend? Are we confronted with a physiological explanation for the Satan concept and associated behaviour?

It is valuable to compare this concept with Paul Levy's Wetiko [7], the curse of evil. Here the parallels are unavoidable: 'who do you think you are?' In what Levy calls Malignant Egophrenia, a bogus identity created by our creative imagination takes over our real nature. It is a psychosis in which we feel 'limited, wounded, having problems or overly grandiose or narcissistic'.

In fact, these are listed (see Chapter 1) as Neil Donald Walsch's 10 illusions of the third kind, the Curriculum Determinant, as: need, failure, disunity, insufficiency, requirement, judgement, condemnation, conditionality, superiority and ignorance. They are part of the illusions that we must navigate; we live in kindergarten for a reason. They are there to serve us, but we must *learn* how to use them. They are merely lessons or tests, apparent problems to be overcome by kindness and mutual help, compassion and action. Love is all there is. Recognising these for what they are neutralises Wetiko.

CONCLUSIONS

The human world in 2020 is locked in Ego Self confrontational attitudes and does not seem to realise its peril. A sensible solution cries out for God Self collaborative efforts to save us from our self-made existential threats. If humanity is on an evolutionary track towards intuition, then we clearly have a long way to go;

conversely, the first steps are clear. Although not absent from McGilchrist's book, the essential emphasis missing from Table 2 and elsewhere is respect, the public face of love. They are surely part of intuition. Can we wake up in time?

REFERENCES

1. McGilchrist, I. (2018). *The Master and His Emissary* (Kindle Location 7). Yale University Press. Kindle Edition.
2. McGilchrist, I. (2012). *The Divided Brain and the Search for Meaning.* Yale University Press. Kindle Edition.
3. Woollacott, M. H. (2015). *Infinite Awareness: The Awakening of A Scientific Mind.* Rowman & Littlefield, Lanham MD.
4. Bernstein, B. (2021). *Discerning Your God Self.* BLB Consulting Inc..; Steamboat Springs, CO.
5. Grosso, M. (2017). *The Final Choice: Death or Transcendence?* White Crow Books, Hove, Sussex, UK.
6. Dossey, L. (2018). Possibilities for Survival of the Human Race: A Global Near-Death Experience. EXPLORE 14(4): 241-247.
7. Levy, P. (2013). *Dispelling Wetiko: Breaking the Curse of Evil.* North Atlantic Books, Berkeley, CA

"Simplistically, those unruly immatures on planet Earth now make really dangerous Frecrackers (H bombs) and the adults nearby became concerned.

Mystically, our Collective Unconscious has called out the cavalry and the Big Guy has responded.

Mundanely, something weird may be happening in some people's minds while most others, if they notice, just chuckle and go their way; 'hidden in plain sight' is a stratagem often seen in Nature and possibly anticipated by the sources of UFOs".

Chapter 7
The Next Breakthrough: OMG, It's OUR Lifetime!

Young First Australian 1969

...we are witnessing in our lifetime something truly extraordinary and important.

There is only Life and Love is key.

The Importance of Sharing for Humanity and its Planet

Consciousness is Primary.
Max Planck

Imagination is more important than Knowledge.
Albert Einstein

SUMMARY

We know that humanity is this century facing at least three existential tipping points: nuclear war, climate change and food and water supply (from population growth and planetary degradation). We speculate on some related aspects of consciousness and emphasise the importance to humanity of sharing.

Some say we may need a real catastrophe (amounting to an NDE) to make us take the drastic steps needed to save our planet. We know within us is a latent collective emotion, powerful if activated by focusing. If we seek within via meditation, as do First Nations Australians, we may achieve collective abilities. NDEs feature contact with transforming spirit entities, as do contact with so-called extraterrestrial (ET) spirit entities associated with unidentified flying objects (UFOs), whose unproven physicality is irrelevant to undeniable evidence that 'something outstanding' is happening worldwide. Any seemingly psychic contact experiences are generally benign and reassuring, linked to powerful telepathic influences, 'good neighbour' help from an unexpected quarter. Philosophers speculate that our entire species will eventually transcend to a more psychic state like that of the Australian First Nations peoples, with universal awareness of the One Mind and its purpose.

We seek possible links between our pressing dangers and what is currently happening to human consciousness. Humanity presently has the collective wealth and know-how to make this entire planet a far safer, happier and fruitful place conducive to the quiet development and introspection we are bred for (see Chapter 5). We know the truth of this facile-sounding statement and that we have enough; all we need is to find a way to share it equitably.

IS THERE SOMETHING WITHIN WORTH SHARING?

If you search the internet with the question 'who are you?' and get past the music references, you may meet another massif of words by philosophers, psychologists and psychiatrists who are trying to define consciousness. If you add 'why are you here?', another layer may offer proselytising words of familiar religious material. But if you add 'Veda', you will find no easy answer: look within. This is the mystic message for millennia to find what we fundamentally share – the probable source of all sacred literature and shamanic wisdom.

SHARING AMONG THE MADDING CROWD

Spectators at ball games (not cricket) will understand the collective mind that soccer fans have called 'footie fever', sometimes dangerously destructive. Psychologists term something like it 'mass hysteria'. But it was the *emotion*, not any behaviour, that was somehow transmitted, and the emotion may be good or bad, or as ugly as in the arena of the Colosseum of Ancient Rome or modern bullfights, surprisingly still surviving. Demagogues are familiar with the emotion and cleverly exploit it. There are contemporary examples; historically, old footage of rallies harangued by Mussolini and Hitler shows the crowd's response.

The same phenomenon was noted (see Chapter 1): something like a collective mind is shared non-locally, but here it is *focused*. It seems that the ability to concentrate on a common goal provides its power.

SHARING IN THE TRIBE

Humanity's mtDNA trail from Africa (see Chapter 5) showed that the N sub haplotype went north via the Fertile Crescent, thence into Europe, Asia, North and South America. Their history – 'ours' for most modern peoples – is familiar. But why did the M haplotype turn south and follow a rapid, less-affluent beachcomber's route all the way to Australia? One cannot deny that the descendants of the N sub haplotype (most of 'us') can be aggressive and dominance-driven. The avoidance and apparent escape south of the M haplotype people, their relict aboriginal descendants' reclusive nature in the jungles of Southeast Asia (despite being first comers), and the frequent rescue of lost Europeans by First Nations Australians suggest a difference.

The first Europeans visiting Australia [1,2] describe a country very different from the desperate poverty apparent at first glance. True, the First Australians had few personal possessions and were described as 'lazy' compared to the Europeans' busy lives; they did not need to work much because there was plenty. The countryside resembled European gentry estates without the grand house: rolling lush pastures and crop fields, some neatly harvested, dotted with trees (from carefully timed use of fire), abundant and easily accessed 'bush tucker'. Crop cultivation, irrigation, tilling and terracing were practised, large dams were built and complex inland fisheries operated. Sophisticated, clean, comfortable domed houses were built in permanent villages numbering over 1000 people and Country was loved, admired and tended. Grain was ground and bread was baked, skins were sewn into clothing.

There is scholarly controversy about whether the First Australians were hunter-gatherers or the first farmers [3].

Sutton and Walshe suggest that the Old People were reluctant to exploit Country because of religious (from the Dreaming) and spiritual restraints. They tended to stay in Country for spiritual reasons. Also, present-day rainfall (much less than then) restricts the growth of modern cereal crops to narrow areas circling the dry centre. Touring such areas by modern car or rail shows how difficult even subsistence farming must have been, with ancient, leached soils. The early settlers generally stayed within the fertile south-eastern states; so it is uncertain how general were the conditions they described.

But the communities were relatively stable and peaceful. Since 1788, European interference has changed much, and First Nations Australians were unable to maintain their ancient culture. As in the Fertile Crescent and everywhere else, there was mainly ignorance and greed to blame for this deliberate dispossession: it was the result of rising population and competition, given the spiritual mindset of Europeans.

The following story [4] is set against that background. It is of a spiritual healing, remarkable in itself, but only partly my purpose. American Gary Holz DSc (1950–2007), materialist physicist and high achiever but emotionally numbed in youth, at age 43 found himself well into a death sentence from multiple sclerosis. By an odd series of synchronicities ('non-accidents'), he was in a jazz club when he was drawn to talk with an Australian woman who introduced him to an Aboriginal healer in outback Australia. The healer, under instruction from the 'Big Guy' (God) and against local custom, agreed to treat him in their home village. The treatment was holistic and familiarly modern: exercises to apply intention by going within. After many months, he was cured and went on to become a healer himself, as he had a gift the Big Guy had a use for.

My point here is the nature of sharing in the community. I illustrate this with the following verbatim quotations from Holz's first-person account. (#Aboriginal healer's explanation).

- 'Sitting quietly in her chair, hands in her lap, staring right through me. I stopped short, at first uncomfortable, then realized she had the same distant look on her face the villagers had when they sat on the ground, staring into space'.
- 'Aboriginal people spend a lot of time in a meditative state – what's sometimes called Dreamtime."#
- 'It's a natural state for us (Aboriginal people), and it's also one of the tools for controlling what we are focused on, and subconsciously attracting'.#
- 'Dreamtime is vital, part of our (Aboriginal people's) way of life."#
- 'Everything that happens in this universe is connected in ways you could never even imagine'.#
- 'Meditation is just learning how to relax, go inside, and listen. If you have a problem or a question, just get quiet, go within, and ask and your inner knowing will provide you with an answer'.#
- 'That's how Einstein got some of his best ideas. He'd just ask, and eventually the answer would come to him'.#
- 'As if in response to my thoughts'.
- 'I suddenly noticed how beautiful (the little girl) was, with her dark skin and big gleaming eyes. She spun around to look at me as I thought that, and her face broke into the biggest grin I'd ever seen. She laughed in delight, jumping up and down. She shyly squeezed my finger, and then ran off giggling'.# 'She says, "Thank you"'.

Before he left, Gary Holz could 'talk' and share in the same way. Other traditional societies may well retain this ancient insight.

IS THE COSMOS TRYING TO SHARE SOMETHING WITH US?

The mention of UFOs is generally still good for a chuckle, but if you sound serious, your mental status is suspect: credibility is still a huge issue. However, there turn out to be several thousand credible first-hand UFO witness accounts involving groups of simultaneous multiple sightings; several authoritative surveys [5,6,7,8,9] leave no reasonable doubt of the existence of *sightings*. The peer-reviewed *Journal of Scientific Exploration* presents more than 30 articles related to UFOs since its first issue (March 1987), some offering everyday explanations but many failing to do so. A more fertile popular audience may have been reached by Shirley MacLaine's (1983) extraordinary *Out on a Limb* [10], whose quotation of the ET Maya is repeated early in Chapter 1 of this book.

UFO performance implies intelligent direction, and their hyper-advanced technology strongly suggests an ET source. This information has been concealed in an unbelievably massive cover-up for some 70 years and muddled by seeming disinformation (see Operation Highjump) but is now gently coming out [11]. I commend the sincerity of the several YouTube video interviews with the key character, Philip Corso (1915–1998), as an old man with nothing to lose or gain except the wellbeing of his children and grandchildren [12]. The frequent (1300+ cases) reports of ground and aerial visual and radar lock-on confirmation, with intelligent evasion or in-station flight accompaniment and vastly superior flight performance – 'only to have the UFO almost impudently outdistance him, there is no simple answer', USAF pilot the late Captain EJ Ruppelt, 1956 [6] – have, well, no simple answer.

The discovery of Earth-like exoplanets showed the likelihood of many billions of possible havens for life forms like ours in the visible universe. Furthermore, the recent revitalisation of the attractively parsimonious (using 'Occam's Choice') panspermia concept (see Chapter 3) makes widespread ET life even more likely. So its existence is no surprise. Star travel has long seemed impossible because light velocity cannot be exceeded but consider the following. Astrophysicist Bernard Haisch [13] co-authored a grant request sponsored by NASA and a major aerospace company [14]; it posits [15] that inertia or mass is an electrodynamic Lorentz field drag from acceleration in the zero-point field, a theoretical source of 'free' immense energy illustrated by the Casimir force. Another NASA group [16] cryptically 'used classical magnetoplasmadynamics on a test article to obtain a (small but anomalous) propulsive momentum transfer via the quantum vacuum virtual plasma'. Photons in optic fibres travel faster than electrons in copper, and Faraday famously 'magnetised a light beam' by altering its optical rotation (Faraday effect). Can we predict what sort of field the following apparatus would generate: multistrand circular fibre-optic coils passing high intensity, coherent, polarised electromagnetic radiation of various wavelengths? These are all possible sources of some strikingly novel UFO technology.

But hard physical evidence for UFOs, the sort you can hold in your hand, is still largely lacking, unless one considers the Roswell artefacts [5]. Lt Colonel Corso says he handled these and covertly passed them on piecemeal for commercial/military development. Lt Colonel Corse also states that he saw four ET corpses that were preserved and autopsied by qualified medical staff whose reports would be fascinating to read. Lt Colonel Corso mentions night-vision goggles, integrated microcircuits, fibre optics, lasers, stealth aircraft, super-hard materials (such as depleted uranium) and the antimissile missile as physical outcomes from the Roswell material. Science historians say these were about to happen anyway, and it was a coincidence that they were in this period and within the tightly closed American aerospace industry rather than academia, where provenance is more transparent. Presumably, these artefacts and the crashed UFO still exist somewhere and will be disclosed when politically expedient. Or maybe not. There is a pot of gold in that mother lode. Also, public reaction would be unpredictable, ranging from panic to outrage at the continued cover-up.

UFO visitation only seemed to intensify since 1947. Simplistically, those unruly immatures on planet Earth now make really dangerous firecrackers (H bombs), and the adults nearby became concerned. Mystically, our collective unconscious has called out the cavalry, and the Big Guy has responded. Mundanely, something weird may be happening in some people's minds while most others, if they notice, just chuckle and go their way. 'Hidden in plain sight' is a stratagem often observed in nature and possibly anticipated by the sources of UFOs.

Are UFOs Real or Are They Just Science Fiction?

The foregoing embodies the very stuff of this literary genre. What are we to make of UFOs? They are too widespread worldwide to be a deliberate hoax but difficult to accept as reality; their literature is copious, and I have been selective. It is also riddled with uncertainty, frank lies and secrecy. Nevertheless, it is clear that 'something very significant is/has been going on'. UFO authorities Hynek and Vallee [17,18] concur that the UFO phenomenon is both technological *and* psychic, that is, physical and mental, although they do not consider spiritual (One Mind) connotations. The best evidence of physicality is extremely impressive and consistent, especially the 42 close encounters listed by Hynek plus the electromagnetic effects and the 'evidence on the ground', including calcined earth persisting to next season. The characters of key witnesses are impeccable, and their sincerity is patent. Still, unimpressed persons cry 'fraud' because ultimately nothing is left 'in the hand'. That sounds familiar to parapsychologists. Hynek was the professional astronomer originally hired to 'explain away' the sightings, and Vallée was uniquely in the loop; the job was often impossible.

Perhaps it is all a mass hallucination, dream or mediumistic experience complete with apports (UFOs), engineered by our collective mind to bring us all together. 'Occam's Choice', and mine, is probably the face value one of Hynek and Vallée (physical *and* psychic). Although it is also consistent with an unassailable power that could frighten us into a collective NDE, such coercion is inconsistent with free will and karmic debt, and the evidence is that UFOs seem careful to keep themselves non-threatening: any choice resulting must be *desired.*

My aim here relates to possible communication with ETs, physical or otherwise, to discern their purpose. Do they have anything to share with us? Interestingly, there is much on record regarding contact experiences, which take one or more of several forms. Many encounters seem intended to be casually noticed in a non-threatening or even friendly way. A survey [19] of 3256 psychologically apparently normal (and truthful) contactees asked 554 questions. Gender, ethnicity (mostly white Caucasian but also African American and others) did not affect the results. Of these subjects, > 75% regarded themselves as 'contactees' not 'abductees'; the contact was non-physical (telepathic) and sighting a UFO was not usual. The experience was 'very real', like an NDE or out-of-body experience; 86% did not want their experience to stop. Any contact was mostly reassuring, egalitarian, helpful, positively transformative, careful to do no harm and to avoid physical contact, all consistent with a 'good neighbour'. The minority of unpleasant contacts can be conjecturally understood as a 'healing', not necessarily the contactees'. I would presume that any ET species smart enough to travel in space would surely have recognised the One Mind long since; our slow-witted species only started this process a few hundred thousand years ago (see Chapter 5). Personally, Hernandez's [19] most significant finding 'supports the unique attribute of the CE [contact experiences] being associated more often with a non-physical entity ("spirit" or "energy being")'.

This immediately shifts us to a different reality. Other entities cited include 'short grey' (unsurprisingly the typical ET form in the film *Close Encounters of the Third Kind)*, tall grey, hybrid, human-looking, insectoid, reptilian, large and small animal, which could all pertain to a non-physical form. Although later and explicitly intending to remedy Ring's paucity of experimental data, the Hernandez report nevertheless reinforces his conclusions.

The late Professor Kenneth Ring, psychologist and noted NDE researcher, was struck by the many similarities between an NDE and a contact experience [20]. In particular, he noted the presence of a non-physical entity and the marked change to 'positivity' of the experiencer in their relation to others, nature and the planet. A personally challenging 'life review' [21] is common to both: the point of the golden rule strikes home. The sobering moment is to realise that really learning from our opportunity is the sole reason we are here on Earth.

However, this was not the entire point of Ring's inspirational Omega Project [22], which is too extensive to summarise here. Fellow philosopher–psychologists speculated on our future evolution via the 'shamanising of modern humanity'. It mentioned the Neolithic revolution as being a cultural evolution, although the more important advance was more likely (see Chapter 5) an Upper Palaeolithic paradigm shift in spiritual perception, possibly an earlier step in our present process. Ring implied a further, more profound paradigm shift: the conscious intent of the Mind at Large (One Mind) is to penetrate humanity's shared mind, to 'awaken the species' [23] to how reality works.

The core message from NDEs and contact experiences is that life continues in a far happier realm after physical death, and experiencers feel they have a mission to pass it on. **There is only life, and love is key.**

But NDEs and contact experiences only happen to some of us, while everybody can learn to meditate. When contrasting experiences with the simple egalitarian example of the tribe described earlier in this chapter, who seem to have achieved a degree of transcendence by habitual meditation, the point of the ancient wisdom of 'seeking within' is considered missed by everybody else. Imagine a society where deception is, literally, unthinkable! Also unacknowledged is the point of the UFOs 'hiding in plain sight'; their function is more likely to be persuasion by psychic means.

Since the end of World War II, there have been signs that persuasion is indeed happening on many levels at once. One of the most striking may have been the Zeitgeist known as the New Age movement [24], which swept the Western youth world in the 1970s with surprising vigour, helped by highly innovative popular music, such as that of the Beatles. Wherever did the New Age come from? Its basis was the perennial philosophy with a Christian slant, and my first contact was the tiny Scottish village of Findhorn exactly 40 years ago (see the first section of this book). It evidently filled a huge need, with a philosophy like that of the tribe outlined earlier in this chapter. Strong support came from copious material received through psychic dictation to Jane Roberts (the Seth books, 1966–1997 [25]) and later Walsch (*Conversations with God*, starting 1992 and ongoing [23]). Crucially influential was the psychic dictation of *A Course in Miracles*, in iambic pentameter (1976), to the atheist psychologist Professor Helen Schucman and her boss Professor William Thetford [26].

The philosophy enshrined in ancestral Aboriginal Australian law (see Chapter 5 and earlier in this chapter), is remarkably New Age in sentiment. All technology has spiritual and social dimensions, tools derived from stone and wood are loaded with moral and spiritual obligation and significance; Elders are the equivalent of senior clergy, judges and politicians; their special respect has to be *earned*. Respect and peacefulness are universal. The economy and spirituality are symbiotic; the here and now is crucial. There is no hiding in a conscious universe, and each part must take responsibility for its actions: therein lies the crux of the laws of karma.

One New Age tenet was the Law of Manifestation (sustained intention), the basis of many current self-help initiatives and books morphing into Lynne McTaggart's internet-based Peace Intentions (see Chapter 5), which are ongoing. An importantly revealing synthesis of spiritual matters; quantum-holographic, universe-wide interconnection; UFO abductions; and the purpose and nature of ETs is provided by Joe Lewels [27]. One may also list the existence of *EXPLORE: The Journal of Science & Healing* and the *Journal of Scientific Exploration*; the Esalen Institute and the Institute of Noetic Studies in California; the huge increase of meditation studies [28]; the TM organisation; the bumpy world trend to gender and ethnic equality exemplifying the golden rule in action; the gradual recognition of post-materialist science; increased interest in holistic medicine and homeopathy; self-healing and healing the planet; the volunteer-run Kindness Newsletter; increased interest in Eastern religions; and finally, the core experiences detailed in Ring's *Lessons from the Light* [29]. Superimposed on many existing good works, these were undreamt of in 1945.

CONCLUSIONS

Ancient wisdom tells us to seek within for who we are. The madding crowd tells us there is something important there, if yet unfocused. The ancient culture of the tribe described above shows us one pathway to transcendence and that our dominant Western culture is so busy with materialism it has forgotten reality; 'If you are too busy to meditate, then you are too busy'. The UFO phenomenon teaches us at least one undeniable fact: **in our lifetime, we are witnessing something truly extraordinary and important**. Whether physical or fantasy (or both), it appears worldwide, and we need to understand it, as it is surely not independent of the One Mind. An earlier generation might have called UFOs 'visiting angels', midwives to help us transition through our imminent self-made peril. An ET ability often noted is strong telepathic influence, a potent modus operandi.

The implications are little short of apocalyptic. We each probably know what is needed, but collectively, we are deaf, blind and dumb; our collective mind is powerful enough to force us to act if it can be focused.

Experiencers tell us that reality is that realm outside Plato's cave, where colours are brighter and Oneness with everything is self-evident. It is long known from mediumistic survival and reincarnation studies (visited during an NDE, OBE or entered at physical death) that it is whence we came and whither we return, hopefully wiser. We all need to go within, listen up and dream of 'sharing'.

REFERENCES

1. Gammage B. (2011). *The Biggest Estate on Earth: How Aborigines made Australia.* Allen & Unwin, Sydney.
2. Pascoe, B. (2018). *Dark Emu: Aboriginal Australia and the birth of agriculture.* Magabala Books Aboriginal Corporation, Broome, Western Australia.
3. Sutton, P., Walshe, K. (2021). *Farmers or Hunter-Gatherers? The Dark Emu Debate.* Melbourne University Press, Carlton, Victoria. Australia.
4. Holz G, Holz R. 2013. *Secrets of Aboriginal Healing: A Physicist's Journey with a Remote Australian Tribe.* Bear & Co, Rochester VT US
5. Corso PJ. 1997. *The Day After Roswell.* Simon & Schuster Inc., New York NY.
6. Weinstein D F. 2001. Unidentified Aerial Phenomena – Eighty Years of Pilot Sightings. NARCAP T04 Feb 2001. http://narcap.org/files/narcap_revised_tr-4.pdf
7. Kean L. 2010. *UFOs, Generals, Pilots and Government Officials go on the Record.* Harmony Books, New York NY.

8. Watts B. 2017. *Australasian Encounters: UFOs Down Under.* Pegasus Education Group, McCrae Victoria, AU.
9. National Investigations Committee on Aerial Phenomena. http://www.nicap.org
10. Maclaine, S. (1983). *Out on a Limb.* Bantam Books, NY.
11. Greer SM. 2017. *Unacknowledged: an Exposé of the World's Greatest Secret.* A&M Publishing LLC, West Palm Beach, FL. http://www.SiriusDisclosure.com
12. Philip J Corso, Roswell & Alien Technology Full Documentary https://**www.youtube.com**/watch?v=EOnroy_3X98
13. Haisch B. 2009. *The God Theory: Universes, Zero-Point Fields, and What's Behind It All.* Red Wheel/Weiser LLC, San Francisco CA.
14. Haisch B, Rueda A. 1999. The Zero-Point Field and the NASA Challenge to Create the Space Drive. https://core.ac.uk/display/10474687
15. Haisch B, Rueda A, Puthoff HE. 1994. Inertia as a zero-point-field Lorentz force. Physical Review A. 49:(2) 678-694.
16. Brady D, White HG, March P, Lawrence JT, Davies FJ. 2014. Anomalous Thrust Production from an RF Test Device Measured on a Low-Thrust Torsion Pendulum. https://ntrs.nasa.gov/search.jsp?R=200000329812018-10-01T00:49:16+00:00Z
17. Hynek JA. *The UFO Experience: a Scientific Enquiry.* 1972 original ed. 2017 New Saucerian, LLC.
18. Hynek JA, Vallée J. 1975.*The Edge of Reality: A Progress Report on Unidentified Flying Objects.* Henry Regnery Co. Chicago IL
19. Hernandez R, Davis R, Scalponi R, Schild R. 2018. A Study on Reported Contact with Non-Human Intelligence Associated with Unidentified Aerial Phenomena. Journal of Scientific Exploration 32(2):298-348.
20. Ring, K. 1993. *The Omega Project: Near-Death Experiences, UFO Encounters, and Mind at Large.* Amazon Kindle Books.
21. Ring K. Golden Rule video. https://www.youtube.com/watch?v=1tiKsKy7lFw
22. Ring K. 1985. *Heading Toward Omega: in Search of the Meaning of the Near-Death Experience.* Amazon Kindle Books.
23. Walsch ND. 2017. *Conversations with God (Book 4): Awaken the Species.* Watkins, London
24. New Age Wikipedia. https://**en.wikipedia.org/wiki/New_Age**
25. Roberts J. 1966-1997. *The Seth Material.* Amber-Allen Publishing, San Rafael CA.

26. Schucman H. 2007. *A Course in Miracles* (combined vol. 3rd ed.) Foundation for Inner Peace, http://www.acim.org
27. Lewels J. 2005. *The God Hypothesis: Extraterrestrial Life and its Implications for Science and Religion.* 2nd Ed. Granite Publishing Columbus NC.
28. Vieten C, Wahbeh H, Cahn BR, MacLean K, Estrada M, Mills P, et al. (2018) Future directions in meditation research: Recommendations for expanding the field of contemplative science. PLoS ONE 13(11):e0205740. https://doi.org/10.1371/journal.
29. Ring, K. (2006), *Lessons from the Light: What We Can Learn from the Near-Death Experience.* Moment Point Press, Needham, MA.

IS THERE A MEANING TO LIFE FOR HUMANS?

Life – What's in It for Me?
Norm A. Verage, Esq.
Man on the street
and most other vertebrates

Life – What's in Me for It?
Viktor Frankl, Auschwitz and Dachau survivor.
Man's Search for Meaning, 1992
www.viktorfrankl.com
and all volunteers, especially firefighters, frontline emergency responders, ambos, nurses, doctors, pharmacists, teachers, police and carers; there are too many heroes to name.

Epilogue – The 'Why' of this Book

In the end, though, all roads, new and old,
on Earth will lead Home, which is not on Earth.

But the journey and hard work mean a lot more
if you know why you are doing it. Keys to the
evidence can be found in this book.

IT'S YOUR CHOICE.

Acknowledgements

I thank Elsevier E.B. for waiving copyright to allow republication as this short, not-for-profit, medical and educational booklet. I wish to thank especially the editorial staff of *EXPLORE: The Journal of Science & Healing* for their prompt help on many occasions. Colour artwork by Barbara Jane Donaldson (nee Cooper, 1956–2014), Canberra. Pastel portrait by unknown artist; purchased 1970, Coober Pedy, South Australia.

About the Author

Peter Cooper is a retired academic with an honours background in chemistry and physics (University of London), whose working life researched and taught about bacteria, viruses and cancer, seeking disease prevention via antibiotics and vaccines. He has worked at medical research institutes in London and Caltech, CA, where he was a Fulbright Scholar. He migrated in 1962 with his young family to Canberra and worked as a Senior Fellow in the Australian National University Institute of Advanced Studies and as Visiting Professor at research institutes in Albert Einstein College of Medicine, NY, University of London, University of Glasgow and University of Oxford. He is past president of his professional society (Australian Society for Microbiology) and past chairman of the Australian Capital Territory Cancer Council as well as being a member of various international committees and editorial boards within his subject area. He is an Honorary Life Member of The Australian Society for Microbiology, the Clinical Oncological Society of Australia, and a National Australia Day Medallist (1988). When not working, he spent as much time as possible singing (English choral), dancing (Scottish country), laughing and enjoying wild nature everywhere within reach.

www.ingramcontent.com/pod-product-compliance
Lightning Source LLC
Chambersburg PA
CBHW041142110526
44590CB00027B/4105